THE WORSHIPPER AFTER THE FATHER'S HEART

ISABELLA OGO-UZODIKE

FOREWORD BY TERRY MACALMON

The Worshipper After The Father's Heart
Copyright © 2013 by Isabella Ogo-Uzodike

The scripture quotations cited in this book are from the New King James Version, Amplified Version and New International Version of the Bible. Emphasis within Scripture is the author's own.

ISBN-10:
0989756009
ISBN-13:
978-0-9897560-0-6

For Worldwide Distribution
Printed in the U.S.A

Cover design: Eagle Entertainment Pictures Ltd
Publisher: Anointed Fire™ Christian Publishing
Publisher's Website: www.afcpublish.com or
www.anointedfirepublishing.com

For further enquiries about the book and our worship seminars, please contact: info@theworshipper.org.uk or visit
www.theworshipper.org.uk

For enquiries about the author's music ministry, please contact: info@isabellamelodies.com or visit
www.isabellamelodies.com

Dedication

This book was borne out of a desire to draw people closer to the Father through worship. This desire was put in my heart by my Friend, Helper and Teacher: the Holy Spirit; therefore, this book is wholly dedicated to the Father, The Son and the Holy Spirit without whom this book would be meaningless. It is the Father's breath upon the letters in this book that will give life and birth transformation in the reader.

Acknowledgments

My husband, Ogo has been my rock and support, my biggest admirer and yet my most genuine critique, my best friend and my boyfriend forever. I thank my husband for seeing and believing in the gifts that the Lord put in me, even when I doubted. There is no way this would have been possible without your unflinching support and encouragement. I love you with all my heart.

Our precious children: Sharon, Stephanie, Shane and Shemaiah who see the best in everything I do, even when it is far from the best. You individually inspire me to be and do better. Each of you are special in your own unique way; you make my life so beautiful, and I am so grateful to God for you. You make motherhood a joy!

My family: My one and only sister, Sonsy who takes it upon herself to support everything I do with so much enthusiasm; I can only say "you're amazing!" And of course, to her husband, Kelly and their beautiful children; my wonderful sisters and brothers-in-love: Pastors Eloka & Marian, Chinwe, Ziggy & Dr. Owei, Nkonyelu & Nze Duru, Ebele & Joy, and of course; all my nieces and nephews. God blessed me with an awesome mother-in-law, Mrs. Evelyn Uzodike. I couldn't have asked for a better family to marry into. They have stood with Ogo and I through the best and worst of times, and I love and appreciate them so much!

I want to also acknowledge Pastors Rex and Florence Chosen for being excellent teachers of the Word. My spiritual growth in the last 13 years has been amazing. I have learnt so much, and what you read in this book is a glimpse of the impartation from their teachings. I also extend my thanks to my loving church family, the Father's House International Church, London; especially the worship team who have helped shape my spiritual growth. I have to make special mention of Chiji and Anna Nwankwo and their beautiful girls for their support.

Amongst the people who have played key roles in my Christian walk are Pastors Chris and Stephanie Oarhe of Hilltop International Christian Centre in Port Harcourt. HICC was my very first church family where my Christian journey began, and they are still my church family when I visit Nigeria and the US. I want to specially acknowledge Pastors Eloka and Miriam Uzodike of HICC, Houston, who have shown me that it is possible to be a people of integrity in our Christian walk. I have so much respect for these wonderful couples.

I really want to acknowledge some awesome worshippers whose ministries have deeply impacted my life and revolutionalised my understanding and experience of worship. I have never met some of them, but their hearts of worship and testimonies have inspired, challenged and motivated me to press deeper in my pursuit of The Father. The first one is a humble gentleman whom I have named 'the David of our time.' His name is Terry MacAlmon; a skilled musician, songwriter and recording artist whose music ministry has impacted millions of lives globally and radically enhanced my personal worship experience. His songs have taken me straight into the throne room of heaven in worship. I have had the privilege of gleaning from his depth of knowledge and wealth of experience from many decades of worship leading across the globe. I count it a great honour to have him write the Foreword to this book.

And then there is the world-renowned Dr. Ron Kenoly, whom I really respect and have had the privilege of sitting under his mentorship. The other is a very down to earth man whom I have never met, but I have followed his ministry over the last few years. His name is Pablo Perez; a recording artiste, skilled player and prophetic psalmist. There are so many others that are too numerous to mention here, whom I have never met, but whose ministries have blessed and helped me tremendously in growing as a worshipper. I want to thank all my friends, family and ministry helpers who have, in one way or another, supported the ministry. My heartfelt thanks goes to my editor, Tiffany Kameni for the many hours spent on editing this book, my proof reader, Susan Effanga and the designer of the book cover, Koya Olusanya. To all the great pastors, too numerous to mention here, who have upheld me in prayers and afforded me the privileged opportunities to minister from their platforms; I truly appreciate you with all my heart. To Cynthia and Marcus of Inner Production Limited, Uvi Orogun of Media Mind UK and Tolu Okeowo of Psalms Records; I say thank you and God bless you all.

Last but not least, I acknowledge my late mother who taught me so much about love, kindness and generosity; but most of all, who instilled in me the fear of God and love for people. Continue to rest in peace mummy. Also to my late dad, who I was angry with for a long time for not being there for me. A deep void was created in my heart by your absence which compelled me to seek after The Father with everything within me. I could never get myself to call you 'daddy' in all the years I knew you, but I can genuinely hands-on-heart say to you: continue to rest in peace daddy.

HEAVEN'S ANTHEM
©Isabella Ogo-Uzodike (2012)

Verse 1
To Him Who sits upon the throne
And to the worthy Lamb of God
To Him the Alpha and Omega
Beginning and the End

Chorus
Be glory and honour, dominion and power
Be blessing and riches and wisdom and strength
Be praises, thanksgiving, prostration and worship
Forever and ever and ever, Amen!

Verse 2
To Him Who was and is and is to come
Who died and rose and lives forevermore
To Him Who holds the key to hell and death
The First and Last Who reigns

Bridge
Hosanna in the highest
Hosanna in the highest
Hosanna in the highest
Hosanna to the Kind!
(Repeat)

Foreword

Twenty-five years ago, I sat in a prayer room on a Sunday preparing to lead praise and worship for the evening service. As I waited on the Lord in His presence with the 40 or so gathered, softly and almost subconsciously, out of my mouth came these words and melody for the fist time: "*I sing praises to Your name....oh Lord, praises to Your name....oh Lord, for Your name is great, and greatly to be praised.....*" No one; especially me, would have guessed the Chief Musician was penning a song through me that would be sung in virtually every nation on the earth over the next several years. The theme of this song is the essence of who I am (who every worshiper is), what I do and why I do it. The who...I'm a singer. The what...I sing praises to His name. The why...because His name is great and greatly to be praised. Worship 101.

Ten years later, one night while sleeping comfortably in a friend's guest room during a ministry trip on the other side of the country, I had a dream about heaven. So vivid and passionate were these images that when I awoke, I immediately grabbed a pen and paper and penned the words, "*Can you hear the sound of Heaven, like the sound of many waters; it's the sound of worship coming from His throne. There are cries of adoration as men from every nation, lift their voice to make His glory known...*" Yet another global song was being shared from the music library of heaven....this time prophetic and eternal in nature. Worship 201......to infinity and beyond!

Fast forward another ten years...I met Isabella Ogo-Uzodike, first by email and then in person. Isabella was the point person for an award I was receiving in the U.K. Upon getting to know her just a bit, I soon realized this handmaiden of the Lord had the same "who, what and why" DNA as myself. I quickly recognized and appreciated the respect and honor she was showing me as somewhat of a celebrity, when, in fact, I was the same as she...a fellow servant and worshiper of Jehovah. She was notably humble in her honoring of me for which I'm certain greatly pleased the Father. After all, true worship and authentic humility are inseparable twins joined at birth.

What I also noticed in this lady was the sense of eternity in her eyes, as she was obviously interested in more than day-to-day life that entraps so many. Her passion for Jesus and His purposes was unavoidable. This is a mark of maturity and selflessness of which the Lord challenges each of us.

With these thoughts in mind, enjoy the pages that follow. Take time and breathe deeply the things of God. Allow the Holy Spirit to truly teach you His ways. We have come a long way....we have far yet to travel in our learning of Him. His discipling of Isabella will help you on your journey. Together, let us press on to know the Lord.

Terry MacAlmon
Worship Leader/ Presence Seeker

GRACE
©Isabella Ogo-Uzodike (2012)

Verse 1
Through every mountain I have had to climb
Through every valley I have had to walk
Through every desert I have had to live
Grace has seen me through

Verse 2
Through every trial I have had to face
Through every battle I have had to fight
Through every burden I have had to bear
Grace has been my strength

Chorus
Grace so amazing
Grace so exceeding
Grace so abounding
Grace by which I stand
Grace so amazing
Grace so exceeding
Grace so abounding
Grace O Grace so great!

Table of Contents

Dedication......3

Acknowledgments......5

Foreword......11

Introduction......19

Chapter One: What Is Worship?......33

Chapter Two: What About Praise?......55

Chapter Three: Who Is The Holy Spirit?......69

Chapter Four: The Lifestyle Of A Worshipper...81

Chapter Five: David; The Worshipper After The Father's Heart......123

Chapter Six: Why Should We Worship?......139

Chapter Seven: Dispensations Of Worship.....151

Chapter Eight: Role Of Music In Worship.......165

Chapter Nine: The Effective Worship Leader. 177

Chapter Ten: Conclusion...Now What?......193

PSALMIST'S CORNER 🎵

IN SPIRIT AND IN TRUTH
©Isabella Ogo-Uzodike (2009)

Verse 1
This is the time
This is the hour
This is the day
The Lord has made
For those who thirst
For those who hunger
For those who wait
Upon the Lord

Chorus
For we will mount up
With wings as eagles
And we will stand strong
And grow from strength to strength
Drink from His fountain
Feast at His table
Here as we worship
In spirit and in truth

Verse 2
This is the sign
This is the season
This is the age
For God's redeemed

Whose hearts are pure
Whose minds are made up
Whose eyes are set
Upon the Lord

Introduction

John 4:23-24- *"But the hour is coming, and now is, when the true worshipers will worship the Father in spirit and truth; for the Father is seeking such to worship Him. God is Spirit, and those who worship Him must worship in spirit and truth."*

Ever since I can remember, I have always loved music; I have always been deeply affected by soul-stirring music. As a teenager, I used to always wonder what was wrong with me because I would break down in tears whilst listening to ballads or love songs. It was even worse whenever I attended church services, weddings or funerals. I would always cry whenever 'love' music was played or sung. There was just 'something' I could not explain that tugged at my heartstrings in a way that nothing else did whenever I listened to 'love' songs. This was a constant source of embarrassment to me as my mascara always ended up running! Apart from ruining my make-up, it was not cool to cry in public for someone trying to protect their diva image, so I would sometimes end up excusing myself to go to the rest room once I felt the tears welling up. It was that bad. So for me, my initial attraction to God and His worship was through my love for music.

As a teenager, I was not into the 'church' thing. I was not mandated to go to church every week, and I definitely was not keen on sitting through hours of boring speeches called sermons; therefore, I stayed well away from church unless it was Christmas or Easter season. Although my maternal grandfather was a Catechist (in other words, a teacher of the Word) in the Anglican Church, and I understand my father was an excellent choir master; I never knew either of them well enough to have been nurtured or influenced by them. My grandfather died whilst I was still a toddler and my parents divorced when I was very young, so I never had the privilege of having a close relationship with my father. Although I did not fully appreciate the impact of this during my formative years, I have come to recognize that growing up in a fatherless household left a deep mark on me which prepared my heart for the Father's love.

Having said all that, I noticed a spooky trend in my life long before I accepted the Lordship of Jesus Christ. I noticed a particular pattern that others around me noticed as well: I was generally considered to be a very 'lucky' person. There seemed to be a force that attracted favour to me in uncanny ways. For example, this trend showed up in frivolous things like wishing for a specific item of clothing; and rather bizarrely, someone would give me specifically what I'd wished for. It happened to me so many times that I lost count of the instances. It was so weird! It is really hard to explain what I mean, but I have since come to understand that the Father was up to something even way back then! Even without knowing Him, He was always so gracious and merciful to me, but I didn't understand why. Well, now I do! He was drawing my attention to Him, even in my filthy spiritual state. I know we can all relate to this one way or another. His mercy and grace knows no bounds.

Why am I digressing into these personal things when this is supposed to be a resource to help others press deeper into God? That's a good question, and my simple answer is...because this book is being written from the heart. This is not an academic or intellectual exercise, but a practical, relational account based on my personal experience and understanding. I fell in love with the Lord, not based on what I read up or what someone else told me about Him, but from getting to know Him for myself. Yes, I refer to scriptures to support or buttress some of the points I am making, but this book does not focus on telling you what to do. The purpose of this book is to share with you my personal journey and the principles that have helped and are still helping my worship experience. I can't tell my story from a distance because it is a personal, unfolding epistle of grace and mercy.

My Christian journey started during the second year of my marriage in 1996, whilst living in Port Harcourt, Nigeria. I was honoured with an invitation to attend a church service on a Sunday morning. As usual, the church music got me tearful, and by the end of service when an altar call was made, I stepped out and accepted Jesus Christ as my Lord and Saviour. I was expecting the experience of being born again to be something radical, like maybe a burning sensation, goose bumps or falling under the anointing; but it was pretty much uneventful except for my usual tears!

That was the start of my Christian journey. I remember feeling elated, and inwardly; I felt so joyous and peaceful. The church people looked so perfect and so joyful. The choir sang so beautifully; people hugged one another and seemed to be so full of love! Everybody looked so spiritual, and I thought, "*Wow! This is the place to be!* This is God's house where everything is perfect, and everyone is flawless, and loving, and caring, and kind, and sinless, and peaceful, and joyous, and everything nice." How wrong I was! This is a misconception that a lot of people have about church people; they expect perfection when, in reality, the church is full of broken and imperfect human beings who have been saved BY GRACE. But that is a story for another day!

Shortly after that, I started to occasionally minister solo songs in church. I remember the very first song I sang in church was "Miracle" by Whitney Houston, although I vaguely remember changing the lyrics to make it more church-friendly. Shortly after, I wrote and sang my first 'official' song titled 'Hero' in church. And from then on, I carried on writing more songs before eventually relocating to the UK in 1998/99.

After being born again, that 'something' which tugged at my heart every time I heard church music became more intense. I got so drawn into the worship atmosphere until I realized that it had become like an addiction. I became a worship junkie! I went everywhere and anywhere if the programme was tagged 'worship event.' I was always craving that atmosphere of worship, but at the time; I assumed it was just my love for music. Now I have come to recognize that it was more than the music which drew me to that atmosphere...I now know IT was the PRESENCE of God; the presence of the Holy Spirit! I fell in love with His presence! There was something so irresistible, so precious and oh so beautiful about His presence that I couldn't get enough of! I can't really describe the feeling, but I know it! It is not head knowledge, but experiential knowledge. I can tell when HIS PRESENCE is present, but I can't describe how I know; I just KNOW! My whole being responds to HIS PRESENCE in a way that is different from anything and anyone else.

After we relocated to the UK in 2000, we started attending a new church, and this ministry was quite young. The Sunday worship was usually led by the Pastor and sometimes his wife, who is the co-pastor of the church, supported by their children. Eventually, I joined the team to sing on Sundays, not expecting what was to happen next. Soon after I joined the worship team with another young lady, the Pastor called us to a meeting and told us to consider who would be the worship leader between the two of us! I looked on in total terror. No, it couldn't be me because I had no experience whatsoever in worship leading, and I had never even been a choir or worship team member! Furthermore, I was pregnant at the time so I would not have the time and energy to commit to such a huge responsibility. I gave all the excuses I could think of and tried to convince the pastor that I was not the right person for the job. Well, let's just say by the end of the meeting, I had a new title attached to my name: WORSHIP LEADER! It was bittersweet, but I have to say it felt good to bear that title even though that I had no clue about worship leading!

To top it all, we had no instrumentalists in church! Backing tracks were used for worship, which meant the song leader had to memorize the sequence and order of the preset backing tracks for all the songs before Sunday service. There were at least six different songs every Sunday. I was terrified; no, I was petrified at the prospect of what Sunday worship would be like! I can't begin to recount the number of times we had to stop singing in the middle of a song to start again because I missed the sequence. I was so concerned about what the people thought about me that every Sunday after church, I would hound my husband with questions such as "Was I good? Did my voice sound okay? Did you like how I sang that particular song? Did Pastor frown when I missed the sequence? Did you notice that Sister A. was not standing up when I asked everyone to stand? Did you see when Brother J. walked out whilst I was singing? Blablablabla..." Let's just say my husband is a very patient man!

I was the Worship Leader who knew nothing about the art or the act of worship. All I had going for me was that I loved the Lord, and I could hold a note (well, most times at least). That was it. Whilst I have a natural instinct for music, I didn't have the faintest idea about keys, pitch, voice control, and so on; neither did I have any clue on the subject of worship. My heart craved worship; every fibre of my being craved for the presence of God because of the beauty of the experience, but I did not have the foggiest idea how to lead myself, not to mention others, into His glorious presence. Now I look back and thank God for everything because that situation forced me to start seeking knowledge and digging deeper into the subject of worship. I read everything I could find on worship and worship leading. My fear or dread of leading worship on Sundays drove me to my knees! I prayed really HARD for the help of the Holy Spirit. In fact, I can remember praying and asking the Holy Spirit not to disgrace me because that would bring the name of the Lord into disrepute. In my heart, I knew the real reason was that I wanted to protect my reputation...as if He didn't already know what was in my heart! He must have been smiling at my feeble attempt to hide my pride behind spirituality!

That was 13 years ago, and here I am 13 years later writing a book on the subject of worship! Over the next few years, I became better equipped to lead worship as my knowledge and understanding of worship increased. Gradually, I became less self-conscious and more confident standing in front of a growing congregation. I became less worried about impressing the people with my vocal ability, and became more focused on developing myself spiritually and getting to know the Holy Spirit more. This book is borne out of a desire to help those who find themselves in the same or similar position as I was 13 years ago. You joined the worship team or became a worship leader by default; not because you particularly sensed the call upon your life, but because there was a need in the ministry, and you stepped in. Or, like me, you were involuntarily volunteered! I have come to understand that, in God, nothing is coincidental! All things are divinely orchestrated to ultimately fulfill the Father's will. Sometimes we may not recognize the call of God upon our lives. Sometimes we recognize the call, but we are not sure how to proceed, or we even resist it because it takes us out of our comfort zone. When God allows such situations to arise in our lives, we must trust His heart; we must believe that He is making all things work together for our good because we love Him, and we are called according to His purpose.

In my few decades on this side of eternity, I have come to the conclusion that human beings, by our very nature, are worshippers. Worship is not something we do, but our worship defines who we are. Everybody worships; it's just a matter of who and what we worship. Some people choose to worship money; some choose career; some choose to worship other people or idols, and some choose self-worship, and the list goes on and on. In this book, we will look at the whats, hows, whys, wheres and whens of worship for those who have chosen to worship the One true God in Whom all things consist. This book will also help everyone from the young worshipper, to the more experienced music ministers, worship team members, choir members and worship leaders alike. I believe with all my heart that this book is also a resource for those who are not necessarily in the music ministry, but for anyone seeking a deeper walk with the Lord because worship is so much deeper and bigger than music. This is a resource for all worshippers. Keep in mind that every believer is a worshipper, so this is a book for every believer! I have also added sections within each chapter called *The Psalmist's Corner* where I am going to share with you some of the songs the Holy Spirit has inspired me to write over the years. These songs are all published and available for download in all the major online music stores like iTunes, Amazon, CD Baby, etc. I encourage you to write new songs to the Lord in your own words, from your own heart as you grow deeper in Him. Additionally, there are prayers at the end of every chapter for those who need them. Even if you decide not to pray the prescribed prayers, I would urge you to say a prayer of your own at the end of every chapter. Do not rush through the book as you would a novel; take time to digest what you have read and ask the Holy Spirit to give you more revelation as you go along.

My prayer is that, as you read this book, the Holy Spirit will give you revelation about the Father that goes far beyond the words in this book. I pray that the Lord will open up your eyes of understanding so that you may feel His heartbeat and grasp the depth of His desire for true worship. I also pray that the Holy Spirit will visit you in a powerful, unforgettable way so that your experience of Him and fellowship with Him will climax and birth a new level of intimacy with Him. I pray that this book will be a blessing and a yoke destroyer in your life so that everything hindering your worship will be removed. I pray that, as you read this book, you will fall in love all over again with the Lord, and your love relationship with the Lord will surpass the love and the relationship you had with Him before. It is my fervent prayer that this book will help this generation and generations to come to worship the Father in spirit and in truth. Amen.

PRAYER

Before you start reading, I encourage you to please pray. Submit and yield yourself to the Holy Spirit, and ask Him to help you see beyond the letter; to help you hear and understand beyond the literal meanings of the text; to open up your spiritual senses to receive fresh and deeper revelations into the Father's ways and heart. Finally ask for grace to implement the changes needed in your life.

For those who are not too sure how to pray, here is a suggested prayer below:

Father, I come to You now in the name of Jesus Christ, Your only-Begotten Son and my Lord and Saviour. I submit and yield myself completely to You as I read this book. I ask that You open my eyes to see what You are showing me by Your Spirit; open up my ears to hear what You are telling me by Your Spirit; open up my mind to comprehend what You are teaching me by Your Spirit. Break down every resistance and remove every hindrance that will limit my knowledge of You and my intimacy with You. My earnest and fervent heart's desire is to know You more and to please You in every area of my life. I am desperate for a deeper walk with You, to know Your heartbeat and to bring You glory in all that I am and in all that I do.

I pray for the grace to make the changes needed as revealed by Your Holy Spirit. Help me to understand the true meaning of worship and learn how to worship You in spirit and in truth. As the potter molds the clay, Father mold me into a worshipper after Your heart for this is my burning desire and passion. Make me a vessel of honour, and a channel of blessing for Your glory. I thank You now because I believe with all my heart that You have heard my prayer, and I receive the answer in the name of Jesus Christ. Amen.

YOU'RE SO BEAUTIFUL
©Isabella Ogo-Uzodike (2013)

Verse 1
Basking in Your glorious presence
Stripped of all of my self-consciousness
Breathing in Your sacred fragrance
Savouring Your sweet embrace

Gazing up on to Your radiant face
Captivated by Your loveliness
Holding on to Your amazing grace
Dwelling in Your secret place

Chorus
You're so beautiful
So wonderful
You delight my heart
Bright and Morning Star

Verse 2
Taking on Your gracious countenance
Liberated from self-righteousness
Unashamed to show my nakedness
No façade and no pretence

Looking on in awestruck reverence

Serenaded by Your tenderness
Unafraid to bare my brokenness
Love so perfect, so intense

I'm so glad that we're best friends
You will always be my best friend

Chapter One: What Is Worship?

Romans 12:1- *"I appeal to you therefore, brethren, and beg of you in view of [all] the mercies of God, to make a decisive dedication of your bodies [presenting all your members and faculties] as a **living sacrifice**, holy (devoted, consecrated) and well pleasing to God, which is your reasonable (rational, intelligent) service and spiritual worship."*

As a baby Christian, I was taught some key principles of successful Christian living that have stuck with me and helped me (and is still helping me) over the years. This is why I feel it necessary to outline the following four key bedrocks of Christian living as a starting point in our study of worship. I was taught to prioritize these four areas as it covers the totality of man's purpose in creation. I have summarised the four areas as follows:

1. **Worship (God):** Worship is really placing God first. Worship is God's priority hence the reason He made it the first Commandment. The enemy covets our worship, and will throw all he can at us to distract us from worshipping God. Prioritizing worship will keep our hearts on the Father and draw us closer to Him. Worship

removes limits from our lives.

2. **Discipline (Self):** Discipline is self-restraint or self-control. Discipline will keep our flesh under subjection and help us mature spiritually to become more like Christ in our character and conduct. God is more interested in our character development than in our comfort.

3. **Ministry (Others):** Ministry is really service to God and others. We are labourers in God's vineyard, and we ought to serve God and one another in humility and participate in Kingdom building. Ministry is about others.

4. **Evangelism (Kingdom):** Evangelism is really spreading the Good News of salvation and championing Kingdom expansion. We have been given the Great Commission to make Disciples of the nations in **Matthew 26**. The Bible says that he who wins souls is wise and we should not be ashamed of the Gospel of Jesus Christ.

This book is primarily focused on worship, but we will find as we go along that all the other areas outlined above are really all aspects of worship!

So what is worship?

There is so much material out there on the subject of worship, but let me start by saying that, in my personal view; worship defies definition as it can only truly be experienced. There is no level of intellectual definition or description that can quite capture the depth, dimensions, breadth, essence and spirit of worship. Why? Because worship is fundamentally a spiritual phenomenon that cannot be contained by mere words, and cannot be grasped by the carnal mind. I repeat what I said before; it can only truly be experienced to be understood. I like how Bob Sorge defined it in his book, **Exploring Worship**. He said that *"worship is a divine encounter and so is as infinite in its depth as God Himself."* I agree 110%.

In the year 2000, I was bestowed with the title of worship leader, but I had no understanding of the concept of worship. I was the song leader alright, and I was tagged madam worship leader long before I understood the meaning of worship. This is the case with many of us in the Body of Christ today. We bear so many different titles, and we assume that our titles have automatically made us spiritual giants and experts in the things of God. We assume that the title begins and ends with our Sunday or midweek worship services when we stand in front of the congregation and proudly display our badges of honour whilst quoting scriptures and looking super-spiritual. Doesn't it amaze you the number of times people come up to the pulpit to lead people in worship, but the focus of their songs is really on 'me, myself and I?' Well, that is not the worship the Father desires, and those are not the kind of worshippers the Father is seeking.

Going back to the question: **What is worship**? I have studied and looked up various attempted definitions of worship; it is worth sharing some of these as a starting point. Generally speaking, the word 'worship' is derived from the Old English word 'weordhscipe' meaning worthiness. In other words, *to ascribe worth* *to something we value.* According to Webster's dictionary, worship is *a service or rite showing reverence for a deity, intense love or admiration, a title of honour, respect etc.* The free Dictionary defines worship as *the reverent love and devotion accorded a deity, idol or sacred object, an ardent devotion or adoration; the act of adoring, especially reverently: adoration, idolization, reverence, veneration; to regard with great awe and devotion: adore, idolize, revere, reverence.* Grammatically, worship is either a verb or noun. In Webster's Dictionary, its verb synonyms include *respect, exalt, prostrate, esteem, glorify and revere* whilst its noun synonyms include *devotion, invocation, veneration, adoration and supplication.*

Webster's Dictionary states that *Worship is to honour with extravagant love and extreme submission.* Worship, in my own definition, is really responding to love overtures from the heart of the Father. I read somewhere, and I can't remember who said this, that true worship is defined by the priority we place on who God is in our lives, and where God is on our list of priorities. I totally agree with that statement. True worship is a matter of the heart expressed through a lifestyle of reverence, submission and humility. In the course of my study, I came across various Hebrew and Greek words, which were translated to mean worship or aspects of worship from a scriptural perspective. I looked up many of these words, and there were somewhat confusing explanations for some of the words. Since this is not an academic exercise for me, nor is it an intellectual essay; I decided not to focus too much on these Hebrew and

Greek words, but to mention them in passing until such a time as I gain a deeper understanding of these words.

The most common Hebrew word for worship is 'shachah' which means *to depress or prostrate in homage or loyalty to God, bow down, crouch, fall down flat, humbly beseech, do obeisance, do reverence, make to stoop, worship.* The most common Greek word is 'proskuneo,' which means *to kiss, like a dog licking his master's hand, to fawn or crouch to, homage, do reverence to, adore.* Both of these terms refer to a posture of obeisance, humility, submission and an attitude of reverential fear. This clearly shows that worship is not about a gathering in a building, a song or the emotional hoopla often associated with large gatherings. Whilst all those can be elements of worship, they do not define worship. It also means that true worship should not be self-focused; the focus and receiver of worship is God.

Interestingly, some of the Hebrew and Greek words translate to mean both 'praise' and 'worship'. Below is some of the text I lifted from Radical Authentic Worship website (www.raworship.com) in my search for the Hebrew words for worship. These words are translated in many different ways: *worship, praise, shout, bless, thanks, sing, etc. Each word has a* different meaning and context in which it is applied.
Avodah - Work, service, service connected with religious duties.
Barak - to kneel or bow, to give reverence to God as an act of adoration, implies a continual conscious

giving place to God, to be atuned to Him and His presence.

Hallal - to praise, to make a show or rave about, to glory in or boast upon, to be clamorously foolish about your adoration of God (as in Hallelujah).

Shachah - to depress or prostrate in homage or loyalty to God, bow down, fall down flat.

Tehillah - to sing hallal, a new song, a hymn of spontaneous praise glorifying God in song.

Todah - an extension of the hand, avowal, adoration, a choir of worshippers, confession, sacrifice of praise, thanksgiving.

Yadah - to use, hold out the hand, to throw (a stone or arrow) at or away, to revere or worship (with extended hands, praise, thankful, thanksgiving).

Zamar - to touch the strings or parts of a musical instrument i.e. play upon it, to make music accompanied by the voice, to celebrate in song and music, give praise, sing forth praises, psalms.

In searching for Greek words that translate to worship, I found these words:

Proskuneo - to prostate oneself in worship; to reverence, to adore; to kiss, like a dog licking his master's hand

Agalliao - to jump for joy, to leap, to exult

Thriambeuo - to make an acclamatory procession, to conquer, to celebrate a victory, to triumph

Sebomai - to reverence, hold in awe

Latreuo or **Leitourgia** - to render religious service of homage, an official religious service

Sebomai - To worship, revere, stressing the feeling of awe

Eusebia - Devotion, to act piously towards

From all the words and definitions listed above, it is safe to say that worship is multidimensional, and therefore, cannot be fully captured in its entirety by a single definition. Worship involves adoration, humility, submission, respect, reverence, obedience, sacrificial service, praise, confession, thanksgiving and obeisance; amongst many other things. Worship is a much richer and wider concept than mere singing of songs in a congregational gathering once or twice a week for a few hours. Whilst worship music plays a really useful and integral part of worship, music is NOT worship. Worship involves an attitude of the heart; and corresponding actions which flow from that attitude to express and convey love. Worship is also an act. For example, in our daily walk, we serve others as unto the Lord. Our very life should flow in a continuous stream of worship.

Worship is really being aware of and responding to God's presence. True worship begins with a deep reverence for God and flows from within the heart. An act of worship without a heart of worship is vain and unacceptable to God. A person can go through the outward motions of singing, lifting up hands, kneeling, waving, and so on, and not be worshiping in their heart. Religious worship is superficial, ritualistic, hypocritical and pointless at its best. **Matthew 15:8-9** captures the Father's thoughts on vain worship: *"These people draw near to Me with their mouth, And honor Me with their lips, But their heart is far from Me. And in vain they worship Me, Teaching as doctrines the commandments of men."*

Our worship should involve all aspects of our life and should flow through everything we do! This is encapsulated in **Deuteronomy 6:5** which says, *"You shall love the Lord your God with all your heart, with all your soul, and with all your strength."* We are three-dimensional beings (i.e. we are spirit beings, we live in a body and we have a soul), and so our worship should engage:

- Our feelings (the emotions - the voice of the body)
- Our reasoning (the intellect - the voice of the soul)
- Our conscience (the heart - the voice of the spirit)

We can only worship God to the extent in which we KNOW Him. In other words, we can only truly worship Him to the extent of our revelation of who He is. There are degrees of knowledge, and our level of worship is in direct parallel to our level of KNOWING Him. Let me break it down further to buttress the point I am making here.

As of May 2013, I can boldly say that I know the Prime Minister of the United Kingdom is David Cameron, and that is a statement of fact. I know of him because I have seen him in the news, read about him in the press, heard him on the radio stations, etc. This is a degree of knowledge, but it cannot be compared to the degree in which the Deputy Prime Minister, Nick Clegg knows him. Although I know of David Cameron, I have never met him face to face; I have never had any kind of physical contact with him; I have never spoken to him, neither has he ever spoken to me. On the other hand, Nick Clegg has spoken to David Cameron; they have probably dined and wined together; they have probably travelled in the same car, and maybe been on family vacations together.

Although Nick Clegg knows David Cameron better than I know him, there is someone who knows David even better, and that is his wife, Samantha Cameron. Samantha shares the same address with her husband, eats, sleeps and talks with him everyday, and they have children together. She knows him intimately, and their lives are entwined. The common denominator here is that we all know David Cameron, but my degree of knowledge of him cannot be compared to his wife's knowledge of him. Whereas I can go about my business on a daily basis without any vested interest in David Cameron's activities, his wife, who loves and cares for him, is most certain to constantly have him on her mind. If she doesn't talk to her husband in the course of the day, it would probably affect her because she would miss him. She would pick up the telephone and call him; she would know his voice, and he would know hers. Why? Because they have a close relationship, they are in constant communion and communication. They know each other thoroughly. They live out of each other's pocket.

I liken this to the worship of the Father. It is based on relationship, not the institution of religion. It is an ongoing lifestyle of fellowship and communion with the Father. It is not a start-stop relationship that is rekindled every Sunday for a couple of hours, and put aside for another six days. It is a 24/7, 365 days a year relationship; a relationship based on covenant, not convenience. For a relationship to be healthy, it needs to be nurtured; it needs to be developed, and it needs commitment. If there is no commitment and investment of time, energy and resources in a relationship; that relationship is weak, shaky, vulnerable and can be easily broken. In such relationships, one can afford to be flaky, insincere and lukewarm. Worship is definitely an area where the phrase 'actions speak louder than words' applies.

I will share another example from my personal life that some of us super-spiritual people may find slightly uncomfortable; nevertheless, I will share it because I believe it helps capture the depth and breadth of worship. I am a married woman, and there is a level of intimacy I share with my husband that I share with no other human being. There is a depth of knowledge he has of me which no one else can attain with me, whilst I am married to him. We have sexual intercourse, and this is an extremely intimate and private experience. I liken this to the worship of the Father. Worship is for Him alone. Worship is like spiritual intercourse when our highest priority is to please and pleasure Him alone. I call it the 'Inner Court *Koinonia*'. *Koinonia* is a Greek word whose essential meaning embraces concepts such as fellowship, communion, joint participation, sharing and intimacy. True worship takes place in the INNER Inner Court also known as the Most Holy Place or The Holy of Holies; past the gates, past the crowds, past the noise and the distractions of the outer court. In that moment of worship, nothing else matters and nothing else gets attention but the object of worship which, in our case, is God, the Father. The Father is seeking for authentic lovers, genuine inside and out, consistent in and out of season!

Now, anyone around me knows that I love my husband because I am always talking about him, always saying wonderful things about him, always praising him for one reason or the other. Well, that's good but what if I did and said all the right things outwardly to give all the right impressions, but then when I get home; I ignore him, don't talk to him, don't care about where he is, don't listen to him, don't attend to his needs, and don't spend any intimate moments with him? Although I may deceive outsiders to the real state of our relationship, he and I would know the truth of the unhealthy state of our relationship. He and I would know that it is all a façade. This is what we sometimes do in church; we play church even with God! Think about it. What is the point of impressing the world with our ability to quote scriptures and appear super-spiritual if we are not genuine in our worship of God? It is pointless!

Relating this back to worship, this is what we call vain worship described in **Matthew 15:8-9**. This is when we have rehearsed the art and act of worship without the heart of worship. You can liken this to casual intercourse where the motions are carried out without the emotions. We simply go through the motions for self-gratification, but we know deep in our hearts that there is no relationship, no close bond, no commitment, no fidelity and no covenant. Thank God that He is so merciful and patient with us. He lovingly steers us back to Himself, and the more we seek Him, the more we know Him; the more we know Him, the deeper and higher our dimension of worship of Him will become; the more we become like Him, the more we begin to think like Him, talk like Him, walk like Him and look like Him. This was God's original plan to make us in His image after His likeness. I believe with all my heart that If we genuinely seek God, we will surely find Him. He wants us to find Him, which is why He has made accessibility to Him so easy for whosoever wills! The Bible tells us in **James 4:8** that if we draw near to God, He will draw near to us.

What about individual versus corporate worship?

I thought it necessary to touch on personal versus corporate worship because, in my few years of ministry, I have observed some practices that seem to confuse private devotional time with corporate worship. I have been in corporate gatherings where chaos reigned because some 'super-spiritual' individual became uncontrollable and therefore, disruptive. It is really important that we understand the delicate balance between being expressive (which is desirable and appropriate in worship) and being excessive (which is distracting and inappropriate) in a corporate gathering. Both private and corporate worship are God-centered, and may consist of the same or similar expressions, but the dynamics are different. Personal worship is a two-way intimate time of fellowship between the worshipper and God, whereas corporate worship has a third dimension, and that dimension is fellowship with others. In this case, a certain level of order should be maintained.

Have you ever been in a corporate worship gathering and suddenly someone jumps out from the congregation and starts prancing around, punching the air frantically and making loud noises? That is a distraction! There is a proper place and time for everything. Corporate worship should be orderly and sober-minded. The spirit of the prophets are subject to the prophets **(1 Corinthians 14:32)**. This does not suggest we should all act exactly the same way in corporate worship. Just as we have different personalities, our expressions may differ, however, everything should ultimately work in harmony to glorify God and edify the church. Our blueprint for corporate worship can be found in **Revelations 4 & 5** where there are accounts of the angels, elders and creatures worshipping God in unison.

Our personal time of worship is between us and God; it is a private time with Him and affords us the opportunity to get intimate with Him. It is our time for personal devotion and may come in various forms: meditation, praying, studying the Word, singing, clapping, dancing, bowing etc. Jesus Christ often withdrew from others to spend intimate moments alone with His heavenly Father **(Mark 1:35; Luke 5:16)**, and we all need to do this regularly as well. There is no substitute for personal devotion if we are to grow in intimacy and knowledge of God. Our private worship time helps us develop spiritually and nurture a deeper walk with the Father, and this builds our faith. There is no substitute for personal time with the Father for any believer.

On the other hand, corporate worship is the gathering

of God's people for the purpose of fellowship and for glorifying God. Whilst all worship is primarily God-centered and God-focused, corporate worship is a time for God's people to bond in fellowship and build up one another in faith and love. Corporate worship is powerful when individual members have spent time in personal devotion and therefore, are spiritually in tune with the heart of the Father. The church is edified when believers worship together in unity and in unison. **1 Corinthians 14** gives sound counsel on conduct during corporate worship. God is not the author of confusion (verse 33) so all things should be done decently and in order (verse 40).

Personal worship affords us the opportunity to shut down and shut out the noise of the world around us so that we may, in the stillness, hear God speak to our hearts. In those moments, we can seek direction from God and enquire of Him what His will for our life is. It requires discipline, consistency and commitment on our part to create the time required to build a personal altar of worship unto the Lord. When we are personally recharged, our corporate worship is powerful, dynamic and edifying. Both personal and corporate worship are fundamental to our Christian walk. Corporate worship attracts the manifest presence of God in our midst **(Matthew 18:20; 2 Chronicles 5:13-14)** and facilitates an atmosphere for the gifts of the Spirit to be manifested. It enhances the feeling of unity within a body of believers **(Psalm 133:1)**, and presents the opportunity to confess and profess our faith before others.

In rounding up this section on the definition of

worship, I daresay; for me, all of the definitions outlined earlier in the chapter are missing the KEY, FUNDAMENTAL, CRUCIAL element of worship …and that is the function and presence of the Holy Spirit. I have dedicated chapter three of this book in its entirety to talk about the person of the Holy Spirit because worship that is not Spirit-led and Spirit-filled is a mere religious event with no life-giving nor life-transforming dimension. It may feel good, sound good and look good, but if it is not Spirit-filled and Spirit-led, it is not worship on God's terms. I believe that if we truly want to please the Father in and with our worship, we must start from two foundational scriptures. To me, these scriptures encapsulate and embody what the Father is looking for in worship and in the worshipper.

The first Scripture is **John 4:23-24**: *"But the hour is coming, and now is, when the true worshipers will **worship the Father in spirit and truth**; for the Father is seeking such to worship Him. God is Spirit, and those who worship Him **must worship in spirit and truth**."* We will break this passage down further as we go along.

The second scripture is **Romans 12:1**, which reads, *"I beseech you therefore, brethren, by the mercies of God, that you **present your bodies a living sacrifice**, holy, acceptable to God, which is your reasonable service."* The Amplified Version gives more insight *"I appeal to you therefore, brethren, and beg of you in view of [all] the mercies of God, to make a decisive dedication of your bodies [presenting all your members and faculties] as a **living sacrifice**,*

holy (devoted, consecrated) and well pleasing to
God, which is your reasonable (rational, intelligent)
service and spiritual worship." The living sacrifice can
be defined as living in submission to God and dying to
the flesh.

I would like to conclude this chapter by looking at the
account in **Luke 7:37-47**:
"*And behold, a woman in the city who was a sinner,
when she knew that Jesus sat at the table in the
Pharisee's house, brought an alabaster flask of
fragrant oil, and stood at His feet behind Him
weeping; and she began to wash His feet with her
tears, and wiped them with the hair of her head; and
she kissed His feet and anointed them with the
fragrant oil. Now when the Pharisee who had invited
Him saw this, he spoke to himself, saying, "This Man,
if He were a prophet, would know who and what
manner of woman this is who is touching Him, for she
is a sinner." And Jesus answered and said to him,
"Simon, I have something to say to you." So he said,
"Teacher, say it." "There was a certain creditor who
had two debtors. One owed five hundred denarii, and
the other fifty. And when they had nothing with which
to repay, he freely forgave them both. Tell Me,
therefore, which of them will love him more?" Simon
answered and said, "I suppose the one whom he
forgave more." And He said to him, "You have rightly
judged." Then He turned to the woman and said to
Simon, "Do you see this woman? I entered your
house; you gave Me no water for My feet, but she has
washed My feet with her tears and wiped them with
the hair of her head. You gave Me no kiss, but this
woman has not ceased to kiss My feet since the time*

I came in. You did not anoint My head with oil, but this woman has anointed My feet with fragrant oil. Therefore I say to you, her sins, which are many, are forgiven, for she loved much. But to whom little is forgiven, the same loves little."

This account opened my eyes to certain revelations about the worship which the Father desires and seeks:

1. No matter our spiritual state, we can come to the Father in genuine love, and our worship will be acceptable to Him. This woman was a sinner!

2. Worship that pleases God involves sacrificial giving. We have to be willing to give up something precious and costly as the woman did in the above account.

3. Worship that pleases God comes from a place of total submission and brokenness. A broken and contrite heart, the Lord will not despise. This woman was totally broken!

4. Our depth of worship reflects the depth of our thanksgiving or our heart of gratitude toward the Father as demonstrated in the parable shared above.

5. We have to be willing and able to suffer the criticism, ridicule and scorn of men to press into His presence as this woman did. We have to be bold in the face of man's disapproval, and we have to be willing to do what others are not willing to do to demonstrate our commitment to and our love for the Lord.

6. True worship is extravagant. Not only did she break her costly oil, she washed His feet with

her tears and wiped them with her hair! She anointed his feet and kissed them! And she did all this not caring what others thought of her.
7. There is a great reward for true worship. True worship captures the Father's attention, and He actually brags on a true worshipper. Read above what Jesus said about this woman in verses 44-47. What an honour!

When we worship with a pure heart and an open and repentant spirit, God is glorified, we are purified, the church is edified and the devil is terrified! I love what Rick Warren said about worship in his book, **Purpose Driven Life**. He said, *"Anything we do that brings pleasure to God is an act of worship!"* I broadly agree with this statement because everything we do in honour of God, directly or indirectly, is an act of worship. So in conclusion, our worship must be Spirit-led and God-centered. In worship, we come to offer something up and to give God all of ourselves and our substance. Our worship is to bring God, who is our audience, pleasure, and not to pleasure ourselves. The sole purpose and essence of worship must always be to please and pleasure God, to glorify God! Worship is God's priority, so the worship that the Father desires cannot be measured by the standards of mere men. God is the one who seeks true worshippers to worship Him in spirit and in truth. He knows what He is seeking, and He knows when He finds what He seeks in us, so we should pause and ask Him to help us become what and who He is seeking, not what men think He is seeking. Selah.

Key questions we need to ask ourselves about our worship:
- Is it scriptural?
- Does it please and glorify God?
- Does it build us up to become more like God?
- Does it edify the Body of Christ?
- Does it draw us and others to God?

PRAYER

Lord, I thank You for opening my eyes, ears and heart to receive Your revelation on the subject of worship. I ask that You help me to become the kind of worshipper that You are seeking. I avail myself to You now; I open up my heart to You right here and right now. Show me Your ways, O Lord; teach me Your paths. Lead me in Your truth and teach me, for You *are* the God of my salvation. I wait on You to reveal Your heart to me so that I may live a lifestyle of worship that is pleasing and acceptable to You. I thank You for answered prayers in Jesus name, Amen.

DRAW ME AWAY
©Isabella Ogo-Uzodike (2009)

Verse 1
Draw me away, away
Bring me into Your chambers
Stretch out Your staff, Your staff
Bid me to enter Your courts

Chorus
Take me to the cleft of the rock
The secret place of the cliff
Rejoice over me with singing
Quiet my soul with Your love, Your love

Verse 2
Draw me away, away
Bring me into Your throne room
Show me Your face, Your face
Under Your banner of love

Bridge
You are holy, holy
Holy full of glory
You are holy, holy
Holy full of beauty

Chapter Two: What About Praise?

Psalm 150:1-6- *"Praise God in His sanctuary; Praise Him in His mighty firmament! Praise Him for His mighty acts; Praise Him according to His excellent greatness! Praise Him with the sound of the trumpet; Praise Him with the lute and harp! Praise Him with the timbrel and dance; Praise Him with stringed instruments and flutes! Praise Him with loud cymbals; Praise Him with clashing cymbals! Let everything that has breath praise the Lord. Praise the Lord!"*

I looked up the definition of praise, and according to Webster Dictionary, it is: *1. Expression of approval, commendation, or admiration. 2. The extolling or exaltation of a deity, ruler, or hero.* In other words, to praise is *to commend, applaud, express approval or admiration; to extol, to magnify or to glorify.* According to the free Encyclopedia (Wikipedia), praise is *the act of making positive statements about a person, object or idea, either in public or privately.* Praise is typically, but not exclusively, earned. Most of the time, praise is really given for something someone has done or achieved. Praise is the joyful recounting of another's positive actions towards us or others. It is closely entwined with thanksgiving, and is inherently universal. By this, I mean it can be applied to other relationships, and not just to God. We can praise our family, friends, boss, or even strangers for noble acts or positive achievements. Praise can be given or offered from a distance, quite unlike worship.

The Free Dictionary defines praise as *"to acclaim, approve of, honour, cheer, admire, applaud, compliment, congratulate, pay tribute to, laud, extol, sing the praises of, pat someone on the back, cry someone up, big up (slang, chiefly Caribbean), eulogize, take your hat off to, crack someone up (informal)."* Praise does not require or place a demand on the **praiser** to know or be close to the person being praised. In other words, praise is merely an acknowledgment of the righteous, commendable or admirable acts of another as stated earlier. Many people ask, "What is the difference between praise and worship?" As Bob Sorge said in his book, **Exploring Worship**, it is as difficult to separate praise and worship as it is to divide soul and spirit. Where does one end and where does the other start? My cautious answer to the question is that praise is really an intrinsic part of worship; it is essentially a gateway into worship; however, they operate in different realms. **Psalm 100:4** suggests that praise is an entry point, *"Enter into His gates with thanksgiving and into His courts with praise…"* Praise is usually an expression of what God has done while worship is a response to who God is. Praise opens the doorway into God's presence (**Psalm 95:1-5**) while worship is responding to God's presence (**Psalm 95:6-7**). It is not easy to differentiate between praise and worship because they are different sides of the same coin; expressions of both could be similar or even identical.

Unlike worship, praise can be offered or given from a distance. Worship is reserved for God alone (**Luke 4:8**), but praise can be applied to other entities. Of course, the praise we give to God is different from the praise we give to others. Praise is relatively easy to offer; worship is not because worship requires that we invest time, energy, resources into developing a covenant relationship. Worship gets to the heart of who we are. To truly worship God, we must submit to Him, and adore Him for who He is, not just what He has done. Praise, as well as worship, is a lifestyle, not just an occasional activity. In church today, we have classified praise as a certain genre of music when the beat is fast, boisterous, high-spirited, exuberant and jubilant; and worship as the slow, quiet, relaxed, meditative, intimate songs that makes us all mushy and soggy. To an extent, the distinctive moods facilitated and conveyed by the different styles of music are not far from the spirit behind praise and worship (in the sense that praise is more exuberant and worship is more subdued), but the point is that praise and worship are more than the music; they are a whole lot more than the songs we sing.

Associating fast music with praise and slow music with worship has certainly more to do with us than with God. As I alluded to in the previous paragraph, the tempo, progression and arrangement of the music definitely have mood-inducing potentials, and can stir up certain emotional reactions; but the lyrical content of a song and the heart from which the song is being offered are more important to the Father than these other factors. I have seen some churches where the worship songs are very fast and boisterous, almost to the point of being frenzied and the worshippers are jerking, shaking, bumping, jumping around and very loud. That does not disqualify their worship from being acceptable to God! The Father is far more interested in our heart's condition than the outward appearance and associated expressions. Praise is scriptural and is indeed an integral part of our Christian walk. The Hebrew word *Hallelujah* simply means 'God be praised' or 'Praise the Lord.' God has done many wonderful deeds; therefore, He is worthy of praise. Praise is fundamentally grounded in thanksgiving and commendation because of an action or reaction that has taken place. The theme of praise is essentially directly connected to what He has done. **Psalm 9:11** supports this as it *reads, "Sing praises to the Lord, enthroned in Zion; proclaim among the nations what he has done."*

Angels and the heavenly hosts are commanded to praise the Lord **(Psalm 89:5; Psalm 103:20; Psalm 148:2)**. All the people of the earth are charged to praise the Lord **(Psalm 138:4; Romans 15:11)**. Everything that has breath is instructed to praise the Lord **(Psalm 150)**. According to **Luke 19:40**, even the rocks will praise God if we keep silent! Praise can take on different forms: singing **(Isaiah 12:5; Psalm 9:11, Psalm 144:9)**, shouting **(Psalm 33:1; 98:4/7)**, dancing **(Psalm 30:11, Psalm 149:3)**, clapping **(Psalm 47:1)**, the lifting up of hands **(Psalm 63:4, Psalm 134:2)**, musical instruments **(1 Chronicles 13:8; Psalm 108:2; 150:3-5)** and words of testimony - the fruit of our lips **(Hebrews 13:15)**.

Prayer, thanksgiving, praise, and worship all flow together. Boasting is an element of praise. When we praise God, we are fundamentally boasting about Him and His works. Praise is usually overt as it is evident and can be perceived (seen or heard) by others; on the other hand, worship can be quite covert, which means that it may be silent and may not be evident to an onlooker. As I stated earlier, we should be cautious about drawing too strict a contrast between praise and worship. However, there is some value in making a distinction because worship goes beyond praise; praise is an integral part of worship, but worship definitely goes beyond praise.

Praise is usually vocal, boisterous, loud, expressive, joyful, and extroverted; whereas worship is usually associated with stillness, quietness, prostrating or kneeling, adoration, etc. The behaviors of worship suggest humility and reverence. Praise can take place from the outer court, but worship is an inner court and Holy of Holies offering. As a note of precaution, please be reminded that the actions usually associated with both praise and/or worship can be identical; therefore, one should not base their judgment on outward postures. Additionally, we should not assume based on all the comparisons made, that worship is nobler than praise. Whilst worship is definitely more intimate than praise, both expressions are integral parts of our love relationship with the Father. Whilst the Father seeks those whose lifestyle and mindset are that of a worshipper; He inhabits the praises of His people! He is enthroned in our praise **(Psalm 22:3)**.

Someone may ask the question, "What are the benefits or advantages of praise and worship?" In other words; what's in it for me? Although the mindset of the worshipper should be to give something, there are immeasurable benefits. Below, I have outlined a few benefits that should serve as some encouragement to us:

1. Praise and worship attracts the Father's attention and therefore, His blessings. In defining worship, we looked at the account in **Luke 7:37-47** about the woman who went the extra mile in worship by anointing Jesus with the costly oil from her alabaster jar. Her actions immediately caught His attention, and her sins were instantly forgiven. That is a blessing!

2. Praise and worship draws down the glorious presence of God and facilitates an atmosphere for the manifestations of the Gifts of the Spirit. Our praise and worship brings God glory, and this is the intended purpose of all creation. In **Acts 2**, the people's worship, in one accord, attracted the presence and power of the Holy Spirit. There is also an account in **2 Chronicles 5:13-14** that confirms what happens when we praise and worship in one accord. *"It came even to pass, as the trumpeters and singers were as one, to make one sound to be heard in praising and thanking the LORD; and when they lifted up their voice with the trumpets and cymbals and instruments of music, and praised the LORD, saying, For he is good; for his mercy endured for ever: that*

then the house was filled with a cloud, even the house of the LORD; so that the priests could not stand to minister by reason of the cloud: for the glory of the LORD had filled the house of God. "

3. When we consistently engage in praise and worship, we are transformed to become more like the Father. As **2 Corinthians 3:18** says, *"But we all, with unveiled face, beholding as in a mirror the glory of the Lord, are being transformed into the same image from glory to glory, just as by the Spirit of the Lord."* Essentially, we grow to become what we worship. Romans 8:29 implies that those who love God will be conformed to the image of Christ. Verse five of that passage tells us that *those who live according to the flesh, set their minds on the things of the flesh; but those who live according to the Spirit, set their minds on the things of the Spirit.* As we imitate Christ, we do what **Colossians 3:10** says: *put on the new man who is renewed in knowledge according to the image of Him who created us.* Praise and worship transforms our minds and sets our eyes on things which are above. **Psalm 115** talks about idols and idolaters; verse eight says,*"Those who make them are like them; so is everyone who trusts in them."* Therefore implying that those who worship them are like them. We worship God so we become like God. This can be witnessed even in our human relationships as well. Do you notice how husbands and wives start resembling each

other when they've been together for a long time?

4. Praise and worship builds our faith. It builds our confidence in God and is a source of encouragement when we go through trials and tribulations. David encouraged himself in the Lord from the account in **1 Samuel 30** when he was greatly distressed after finding out that he lost everything, including his family. On top of that, the people were so angry with him that they were threatening to stone him, but David encouraged himself in the Lord.

5. Praise and worship are the highest forms of spiritual warfare. In **2 Chronicles 20**, Jehoshaphat appointed singers to lead his army into battle with praise unto the Lord. When they went into battle singing and praising God, the Lord set an ambush, and their enemies were defeated. Read the account below of what Jehoshaphat did when he received the threat:

"*And Jehoshaphat bowed his head with his face to the ground, and all Judah and the inhabitants of Jerusalem bowed before the Lord, worshiping the Lord. Then the Levites of the children of the Kohathites and of the children of the Korahites stood up to praise the Lord God of Israel with voices loud and high. So they rose early in the morning and went out into the Wilderness of Tekoa; and as they went out, Jehoshaphat stood and said, "Hear me, O Judah and you inhabitants of Jerusalem: Believe in the Lord your God, and you shall be established; believe His prophets, and you shall prosper." And when he had consulted with the people, he appointed those who should sing to the Lord, and who should praise the beauty of holiness, as they went out before the army and were saying: "Praise the Lord, For His mercy endures forever." Now when they began to sing and to praise, the Lord set ambushes against the people of Ammon, Moab, and Mount Seir, who had come against Judah; and they were defeated. For the people of Ammon and Moab stood up against the inhabitants of Mount Seir to utterly kill and destroy them. And when they had made an end of the inhabitants of Seir, they helped to destroy one another."*

There is a story in **Joshua 6** where the Lord instructed the Israelites in Jericho on what to do. They diligently obeyed the Lord and marched around the city for six days. On the seventh day; after they'd marched around the city seven times, they shouted (which is a form of praise) as instructed, and the walls of Jericho came tumbling down. It was then that they took the city! See verse 20 below:

" So the people shouted when the priests blew the trumpets. And it happened when the people heard the sound of the trumpet, and the people shouted with a great shout, that the wall fell down flat. Then the people went up into the city, every man straight before him, and they took the city."

Below is another account about what prayers, praise and worship can do in the lives of believers when we choose to spend time in God's presence. The next account is in **Acts 16** when Paul and Silas were thrown in prison in Macedonia. See verses 25-26 below:

" But at midnight Paul and Silas were praying and singing hymns to God, and the prisoners were listening to them. Suddenly there was a great earthquake, so that the foundations of the prison were shaken; and immediately all the doors were opened and everyone's chains were loosed."

Remember these men were not just casually thrown in prison; they were tied up and were put into the inner prison, but nothing could stop their prayers, praise and worship from reaching heaven, and no one could stop the hand of God from locating and rescuing them! Not only were they rescued, the prisoners got baptised because they saw the power of God at work. They were convicted by the Holy Spirit. This is the power of praise and worship!

I share these stories to ensure we have a balanced view of the essence and power of praise and worship. Praise is just as indispensable in our Kingdom journey as worship. In comparing and contrasting praise and worship, there should be no strict separation of the two. You cannot isolate one from the other; they flow together to the glory of the One whom we praise and worship. Sometimes the distinctions we make between praise and worship are just a matter of semantics. We are creatures of habits, and we have our individual preferences and styles; therefore, we prioritize what we prefer.

PRAYER

Lord, forgive me for the countless times I have failed to praise You and thank You in all situations and circumstances. Help me to consistently make Your praise and Your worship a priority in my life and to always remember Your faithfulness in all situations. Help me to be an instrument of Your praise, even in times when I don't feel like praising. Please help me Holy Spirit to be an atmosphere changer as I carry Your presence and Your power within me. I will praise You O Lord, with my whole heart; I will praise You for Your loving kindness and tender mercies. I thank You for answered prayers in Jesus name. Amen.

SING MY PRAISE TO YOU
©Isabella Ogo-Uzodike (2009)

Verse 1
From the rising of the sun, I'll praise You
To the setting of the same, I'll praise You
From the dawning of the morn, I'll praise You
To the glowing moonlight shade, I'll praise You

Chorus
For Who You are to me,
I lift my voice to You
For what You've made of me
I'll sing my praise to You
My praise to You
My praise to You
I'll sing my praise to You

Verse 2
When I'm on the mountain top, I'll praise You
Even in the valley deep, I'll praise You
When I'm joyful in my soul, I'll praise You
Even when the billows roll, I'll praise You

Bridge
In and out of seasons
There will always be a reason
To sing my praise to You

Chapter Three: Who Is The Holy Spirit?

John 16:13- *"However, when He, the Spirit of truth, has come, He will guide you into all truth; for He will not speak on His own authority, but whatever He hears He will speak; and He will tell you things to come."*

I remember shortly after getting born again, there was so much talk about the Holy Spirit, and I used to really wonder what all the farce was about. To be honest, it was all spooky stuff to me, especially when the term 'Holy Ghost' was used. The mention of ghost always reminded me of the programme 'Haunted House' or the cemetery! Furthermore, I wasn't that keen on having a helper who was stalking me 24/7! Especially when I knew in my heart that there were many skeletons in my cupboard! My initial thought on the Holy Spirit was that 'it' was an angel. As a child, I was told stories about nice and helpful angels, so I just assumed that this Holy Spirit must be an angel, and I used to refer to the Holy Spirit as 'it.' Many Christians still think of the Holy Spirit with the mindset of fairies as told in fables. My prayer is that this book will dispel those myths and bring an eternal revelation of Who He truly is to those seeking to know Him better.

Over the years, I have come to learn so much about the Holy Spirit, and more importantly, I have fallen totally in love with Him, His personality and His presence. I have come to understand that I need His help every moment of the day, in every situation, and that He is indispensable in my life as a Christian. Without His influence, leading, guidance, counsel, help, comfort and PRESENCE; life is meaningless and our worship is pointless, hence the reason I have dedicated a whole chapter to introduce Him properly.

So who is the Holy Spirit?

The Holy Spirit is a Person. I repeat for emphasis: **The Holy Spirit is a Person** included in the Trinity, which is made up of three distinct persons: The **_Father_**, the **_Son_**, and the **_Holy Spirit_**. The Holy Spirit is identified as a Person with a self-identity different from both the Father, and the Son. The Godhead is three-in-one. The Father, Son and Holy Spirit are three; and yet they are one. This is the mystery of the Trinity. Each person is 100% distinct, and yet the sum total of the three is not 300%, but 100%. They are ONE, distinctly three unique persons and yet inseparable. The Holy Spirit has the attributes of a person.

What are the attributes of persons?
A person has:
- A mind - able to think and act upon their thinking
- A will - self-identity, willpower, resolve

- Emotions - feelings and cognitive reactions

As persons, we all have the qualities above because we are alive. A person is identified as a self-conscious being, cognizant of its own existence and the existence of others. A person has a self-identity and a will. Having a will means we have the ability to reason and make a choice about our actions and reactions in any given situation. These are the qualities we associate with self-consciousness, and self-consciousness is exclusive to persons. The Holy Spirit (the Spirit of God) is a person with these qualities.

- The Holy Spirit has a **Mind**:

Romans 8:27: *Now He who searches the hearts knows what the <u>mind</u> of the Spirit is, because He makes intercession for the saints according to the will of God.*

- The Holy Spirit has a **Will**:

1 Corinthians 12:11: *But one and the same Spirit works all these things, distributing to each one individually as He <u>wills</u>.*

- The Holy Spirit has **Emotions**:

Ephesians 4:30: *And do not <u>grieve</u> the Holy Spirit of God, by whom you were sealed for the day of redemption.* Grief is an emotion.

The Holy Spirit is the Executor of the Father's will. He is co-Creator of the universe **(Genesis 1:2)**; the Author of divine scripture, and the generator of Christ's humanity. Just like the Father and the Son, the Holy Spirit is eternal. The Holy Spirit possesses the nature of God the Father such as supremacy, omniscience, omnipresence, omnipotence and eternality because He is the Spirit of the Father. The Holy Spirit is not an angel; He is the Spirit of God; He is God! I am sure some people will gasp in horror at that statement, but let's consider the account in **Acts 5: 3-4** where Peter confronts Ananias as to why he lied to the Holy Spirit, and tells him that he had "not lied to men, but to God." It is a clear declaration that lying to the Holy Spirit is lying to God. There are many more examples in the Bible where the Father refers to 'we' or 'us.' Example: *Let US make man in our image, after OUR likeness...***(Genesis 1:26)**.

God is all-knowing so His Spirit is all-knowing! **1 Corinthian 2:10-11** says, *"For the Spirit searches all things, yes, the deep things of God. For what man knows the things of a man except the spirit of the man which is in him? Even so no one knows the things of God except the Spirit of God."* The Holy Spirit cannot be separated from God because He is God. Yes, I said it again. To the believer, the Holy Spirit was given to dwell inside those who receive Jesus Christ as Lord and Saviour, in order to produce and develop Godly character in the life of that believer. We cannot develop godly character by our own efforts or power; we have to depend on the help of the Holy Spirit to develop His fruit in our lives, and they are love, joy, peace, patience, kindness, goodness, faithfulness, gentleness and self-control **(Galatians 5:22-23)**. Christians are to walk in the Spirit **(Galatians 5:25)**, and be filled with the Spirit **(Ephesians 5:18)**. And the Holy Spirit gives His Gifts and empowers Christians to perform ministerial duties that promote spiritual growth among Christians **(Romans 12; 1Corinthians 12; Ephesians 4)**. He reveals God's will and God's truth to people **(John 16:13)**. He bears witness of Jesus Christ **(John 15:26, 16:14)**. To the unbeliever, the Holy Spirit convicts their hearts by causing them to recognize how sinful they are, so they recognize their need for God's forgiveness and salvation.

We cannot claim to be 'sons of God' if we are not led by the Spirit of God. **Romans 8:14** says, *"For as many as are led by the Spirit of God, these are sons of God."* Many of us know and sing songs about the Holy Spirit, calling Him our best friend, teacher, helper, comforter, and counselor; and yet, we sometimes live our lives as though He does not exist. We have all been there, and it is very easy to ignore the Holy Spirit because we cannot physically see Him. We live in a world where there is a lot of noise surrounding us; where there are so many issues and things contending for our attention. Even as ministers of the Gospel, we are crowded by responsibilities, and we sometimes fail to nurture our relationship with the Holy Spirit due to our 'busyness.' It is very hard to create time for the Holy Spirit when we are constantly in motion. I certainly struggle to create the time to be alone in the presence of God because there is always something going on in my household. I have a very busy household with four children, a full-time job, ministerial responsibilities, family, etc. It is very easy to relegate the Holy Spirit to the background and expect Him to understand because, after all, He knows our heart! We all need to read the whole of **Romans 8** to help us here.

I have used all sorts of excuses to sometimes justify my acts and actions of disobedience to the Father. There have been times when the Holy Spirit has chastised me for prioritizing a whole lot of other things before HIM; those times when I become complacent about spiritual matters because I am too selfish to bring my flesh under subjection. I remember clearly one night when I was happily typing away on FaceBook, sharing some deep spiritual statuses about The Father; nevertheless, I was startled when I sensed the Holy Spirit's displeasure. I couldn't immediately place my finger on what was wrong; after all, I was 'busy' doing my Father's work on FaceBook. In my mind, I could justify spending three hours on FaceBook because I was telling others about Him! What the Holy Spirit dropped in my heart made me pause and quickly log off. I had ignored Him all day, had not even spoken a word to Him, and I had not even acknowledged His presence; I basically treated Him like He didn't exist. Yet, here I was being Miss Spiritual Counselor. Sound familiar? We need to repent! We need to stop ignoring Him and remembering Him only when we want or need something from Him.

I have been guilty of spending hours on a telephone call, catching up on all the latest gossip, but too tired and too sleepy to spend ten minutes talking to Him. I know I am not the only one this happens to, and I believe the Holy Spirit wanted me to share this to show that we all go through challenges, but He desires more than we are currently giving. We sometimes place a higher value on the voice of men than on His voice; in fact, we sometimes allow the noise of religion to drown out His voice and deaden our conscience. He knows we sometimes become so desensitized by the world's system that we can't tell the difference between His voice, our voice and even the enemy's voice. He knows our weaknesses and struggles, and He is calling us back to a place of fellowship and intimacy today.

I have said all that to say this...our relationship with the Holy Spirit is the bedrock of our Christian journey and our worship experience. There is no getting away from this truth. If we desire a richer, deeper and better worship experience with the Father, the answer lies in our relationship with the Holy Spirit. We have to go through the school of the Holy Spirit, learn to listen to Him, learn to recognize His voice, and learn to discern between things which are beneficial versus things which are harmful to our relationship with Him. He has feelings; we need to learn to do those things that will not hurt His feelings. We need to learn to habitually rely on Him and enquire of Him before we make decisions. We have to be passionate and protective of our relationship with Him.

Some people have questioned the relevance of praying in tongues for Christians; in other words, praying in the Spirit. They have said they find it awkward and embarrassing, so they avoid it at all costs. Let me categorically say this: Whoever desires to be a worshipper after the Father's heart must pray by the Spirit of God. Otherwise, they are limited in their fellowship with the Father. There are depths and dimensions we cannot attain in our own strength and understanding; it does not matter how much or how long we pray! We NEED the Holy Spirit. Without Him, our efforts at intimacy with the Father are shallow at best! Period. **Romans 8:26** reads, *"Likewise the Spirit also helps in our weaknesses. For we do not know what we should pray for as we ought, but the Spirit Himself makes intercession for us with groanings which cannot be uttered."* Remember that it is the Holy Spirit who will give utterance; we just need to trust that He knows what we need to pray to the Father about. He knows the Father's Will because He is One with the Father; He is the Spirit of God!

I have watched a lot of Kathryn Kuhlman's videos, and it always fascinates me how she speaks about the Holy Spirit with such fervency. Her eyes, her face and her whole being lights up when she starts speaking of the Holy Spirit; her passion and exuberance are evident, and her countenance says it all. You can almost touch the authenticity of her words. No wonder she had such a powerful ministry. You can't be passionate about worship and not be passionate about the Holy Spirit. It is HIS PRESENCE that makes it true worship! It is HIS PRESENCE that makes the difference. The anointing of the Holy Spirit is what changes the atmosphere and transforms lives. He knows the mind of the Father, so He can align us to move according to the Will of the Father.

There are so many misconceptions about the Holy Spirit that need to be dispelled. Some people have said that the Holy Spirit is a dove. No, He is NOT a dove. **Matthew 3:16** states, *"When He had been baptized, Jesus came up immediately from the water;*

and behold, the heavens were opened to Him, and He saw the Spirit of God descending like a dove and alighting upon Him." Yes, the dove is often used as a symbol of the Holy Spirit, but the Holy Spirit is not a dove.

Some have said that the Holy Spirit is the wind. No, He is NOT the wind. **Acts 2:1-4** says, *"When the Day of Pentecost had fully come, they were all with one accord in one place. And suddenly there came a sound from heaven, as of a rushing mighty wind, and it filled the whole house where they were sitting."* I have yet to see a scripture that substantiates the Holy Spirit being a wind. The wind may be indicative of the presence and power of the Holy Spirit, but wind is not a person. The Holy Spirit is a Person.

Some have said that the Holy Spirit is a fire. No, He is NOT a fire. **Acts 2:3** states, *"There appeared to them divided tongues, as of fire, and one sat upon each of them. And they were all filled with the Holy Spirit and began to speak with other tongues, as the Spirit gave them utterance."* There are instances in the Bible where fire came down and consumed the sacrifices offered to God in the Old Testament; but again, the Holy Spirit is likened to fire which consumes, refines and purifies; but He is not fire. There are many other symbols associated with the Holy Spirit such as wine, rain, water, river and oil. Whilst these are all symbols that could be used in an attempt to describe and portray the acts, functions and/or evidence of the presence of the Holy Spirit; let us always remember that the Holy Spirit is a person, NOT any of these symbols.

PRAYER

Sweet Holy Spirit, my Helper and my Comforter, I acknowledge Your indwelling and infilling presence in me. I truly appreciate and value You, and I do not take You for granted. Help me to always be conscious of Your presence; forbid me from doing, saying, or thinking anything that will offend You in anyway. Please help me to be pleasing to the Father in all my ways. I cannot do it by myself; I need You every single moment of my life. Enlighten, guide, strengthen and teach me what I ought to do and constrain me to do it. Help me to be submissive in everything that You permit to happen to me; reveal to me The Father's will for my life. I thank You for answered prayers in Jesus name. Amen.

HOLY SPIRIT GENTLE SPIRIT
©Isabella Ogo-Uzodike (2009)

Verse 1
Holy Spirit, Gentle Spirit
You are welcome in this sanctuary
Let Your presence
Fill this worship atmosphere
Reveal the Father's heart
Perform the Father's will

Verse 2
Holy Spirit, Gentle Spirit
You are welcome in this tabernacle
Let Your fragrance
Fill this worship atmosphere
Reveal the Father's heart
Perform the Father's will

Verse 3
Holy Spirit, Gentle Spirit
You are welcome in this Holy Temple
Let Your glory
Fill this worship atmosphere
Reveal the Father's heart
Perform the Father's will

Verse 4

Holy Spirit, Gentle Spirit
You are welcome in this yielded vessel
Let Your power
Fill this worship atmosphere
Reveal the Father's heart
Perform the Father's will

Chapter Four: The Lifestyle Of A Worshipper

Romans 8:13-14- *"For if you live according to the flesh you will die; but if by the Spirit you put to death the deeds of the body, you will live. For as many as are led by the Spirit of God, these are sons of God."*

What should a worshipper's lifestyle be like? This is a question that is constantly on my mind, and rightly so. This question should stay on the consciousness of anyone who genuinely desires fellowship with the Father. In the world we live, the line is sometimes blurry between the saved and the unsaved because, after all, we have an excuse: we are HUMAN! We sometimes conveniently brush the quiet voice of our conscience aside with excuse after excuse until we stifle that voice out of our consciousness.

I can think of a thousand times when I have wilfully done the wrong thing and tried to justify it by giving it a righteous twist. Oh, I lied to Mary because Martha wanted me to, and I didn't want to hurt anyone's feelings. The Holy Spirit has convicted me many times about what we call harmless lies. He has convicted me of the times I spent a couple of hundred pounds on an item, and when my husband asked me about the price, I offhandedly said something like, "It was only £40 on sale..." "It's a harmless lie," I'd say to myself. "After all, no one's been hurt." There have been many occasions when I've been in a store and the store assistant/cashier either gave me too much change or forgot to scan an item before putting it in my bag. There were times when I conveniently looked away, and pretended I didn't notice; and there were times when I actually had the nerves to call it God's favour. Other times we tell half-truths (which are full-lies, by the way) and call it 'using wisdom!'. We know who the father of all lies is, and it definitely is not God! We must remember that God will not break His own Word because that would mean that He would sin against Himself! God will not back sin, but He will forgive us when we humble ourselves and repent.

Let's look at the definition of lifestyle. The Free Dictionary defines lifestyle as: *a way of life or style of living that reflects the attitudes and values of a person or group.* The definition of lifestyle simply means the typical way a person goes about living their lives daily. A lifestyle is made up of habits we form over time. Tryon Edwards captures this well when he said, "*Thoughts lead on to purposes; purposes go forth in action; actions form habits; habits decide character; and character fixes our destiny.*" Thoughts become actions; actions become habits; habits become character, and character becomes lifestyle. Our lifestyles then define who we are. It is true that we are not what we do, but what we do springs out of who we are. Remember, as a man thinks, so is he. As Jesus said, what defiles a man is not what goes in, it's what comes out.

Now that we have looked at the definition of lifestyle, the question is: What should a worshipper's lifestyle be like? Have you ever been in situations where you know someone in church as a 'worship leader,' a 'prophet/prophetess' or any other exalted titles we care to give ourselves? In church, they are so spiritual, polite, courteous, and anointed; but when you see the same person outside church, you can't help but wonder, "WHAT WENT WRONG?!!!" Better yet, let's get personal here. Are you the awesome, anointed vessel who brings down heaven during a Sunday service, but dishes out hell from Monday to Saturday? We all need to look in the mirror and be honest with ourselves about what we see. This is not about finger pointing or bringing condemnation, but about bringing conviction. I pray this conviction will birth a godly transformation in our lives, churches and communities. The Lord has not called us to do and be like Him only whilst on the platforms or pulpits on Sundays; He wants us to do and be like Him everyday! He has not called us to talk the talk without walking the walk. We ought to be doers and not hearers only. He is calling us to a place of consecration, which is separation from the world.

Of course, the most obvious lifestyle of a worshipper is that they actually worship; a worshipper is one who habitually spends quality time in acts of worship. A worshipper will regularly and consistently create time to praise and worship God, both privately and publicly. That is the basic lifestyle of a worshipper! Below are some of the key qualities that depict the lifestyle of a worshipper.

1. Love

Love is the foundation of our Christian Faith. God is LOVE. Love and God cannot be separated! **1 John 4:7-8** puts it this way, *"Beloved, let us love one another, for love is of God; and everyone who loves is born of God and knows God. He who does not love does not know God, for **God is love**."* The Bible has so much to say about love, so let's start with a definition of the love we are speaking about here. There are various Greek words for love, but our focus is on AGAPE, the God kind of love. It is a love that is selfless, sacrificial and unconditional. Worship is love in expression, so a worshipper is basically a lover of God and His people. Love rejoices in giving, and chooses to forgive even when wronged. **John 3:16** says, *"For God so loved the world, that he GAVE His only begotten Son, that whosoever believeth in Him should not perish, but have everlasting life."*

This love does not seek after its own and is without hypocrisy. The love we speak about is different from the love promoted in the society we live in where everything is about 'me, myself and I.' I was watching a programme where mothers were teaching their little girls to chant "it's all about me!!!" They were priming these beautiful young children to become future beauty queens, and this was part of their preparation. The message was basically self-promotion and self-gratification. This is rife, even in ministry; it's 'my ministry, my gift, my church, my pulpit, my my my... me me me.' I was having an interesting conversation with my husband recently about some of the cases we had been dealing with in marriage counseling, and we came to a startling conclusion; every broken relationship or fellowship is rooted in selfishness, the very opposite of the love we speak about. Everyone is looking out for "number one." Consequentially, love for others is pushed down the priority ladder.

As true worshippers, the footprints and fingerprints of love should be plastered all over our life stories and relationships; our actions should reflect that which we profess. We have to choose love in every situation. Of course, this is much easier said than done. As human beings, there is no one that is perfect; not one. We all make mistakes; we will offend each other at times; we will upset people and people will upset us. Many people say, "Life happens," but the qualities that will set us apart from the world is how we choose to act or react when these inevitable things happen. Isn't it almost comical when we come across people who call themselves ministers of the Gospel; in other words, they have been called into the ministry of reconciliation, yet they are in conflict with almost everyone around them? That is contradiction epitomized! Sometimes we hide behind spirituality when all that is required is a simple attitude change and a little dose of love. I heard a Pastor say that the meanest, most unforgiving people he had ever met in his life were church folks who claim to love God, yet they harbor hatred for others. The Bible tells us in **1 John 4:20-21:** *"If someone says, "I love God," and hates his brother, he is a liar; for he who does not love his brother whom he has seen, how can he love God whom he has not seen? And this commandment we have from Him: that he who loves God must love* *his brother also."* Have you ever heard the phrase 'Love is as love does?' Well, it's true. And this applies to worship too; a worshipper is as a worshipper does!

We are commanded to love one another in **John 15:12.** *"This is My commandment, that you love one another as I have loved you."* And in **John 13:35** Jesus said, *"By this all will know that you are My disciples, if you have love for one another."* Based on what Jesus said here, love is what sets us apart from the world; 'loving' is how everyone will know that we are disciples of Jesus Christ! The ultimate definition of the love we speak about is found in **1 Corinthians 13:1-13:**

"Though I speak with the tongues of men and of angels, but have not love, I have become sounding brass or a clanging cymbal. And though I have the gift of prophecy, and understand all mysteries and all knowledge, and though I have all faith, so that I could remove mountains, but have not love, I am nothing. And though I bestow all my goods to feed the poor, and though I give my body to be burned, but have not love, it profits me nothing. Love suffers long and is kind; love does not envy; love does not parade itself, is not puffed up; does not behave rudely, does not seek its own, is not provoked, thinks no evil; does not rejoice in iniquity, but rejoices in the truth; bears all things, believes all things, hopes all things, endures all things. Love never fails. But whether there are prophecies, they will fail; whether there are tongues, they will cease; whether there is knowledge, it will vanish away. For we know in part and we prophesy in part. But when that which is perfect has come, then that which is in part will be

done away. When I was a child, I spoke as a child, I understood as a child, I thought as a child; but when I became a man, I put away childish things. For now we see in a mirror, dimly, but then face to face. Now I know in part, but then I shall know just as I also am known. And now abide faith, hope, love, these three; but the greatest of these is love."

These are profound words! These standards are impossibly high for mere mortals to attain without the help of the Holy Spirit; so once again, it boils down to how much we are willing to yield ourselves to the prompting and leading of the Holy Spirit in us. Even the noblest of us have to rely on the Holy Spirit because we are not naturally wired to be this selfless, and the environment we live in makes it even harder to be selfless. Even at our very best, our self-righteousness is as filthy rags before God. Love requires us to season what we think, say and do with grace. How we treat other people matters; how we speak to people matters; how we react to offences matter; even what we think matters. People will sometimes take our love for granted; people will sometimes abuse and betray the love we so graciously offer; people will sometimes reject the love we offer, but the God principle of love says, "Keep loving!" If we find that we have been hurt so much that our hearts have become hardened, what should we do? You guessed right! Ask the Holy Spirit to help us! It is not by our might, nor by power; but by the Spirit of God.

One who seeks after the Father's heart has to love extravagantly. The first commandment is to love

(Mark 12:30); the greatest gift is love **(1 Corinthian 13:13).** Against this, there is no law. This means we can never go wrong with love. Even when it seems like we lost, we have still won because we loved in spite of! We obeyed the Word of the Father even when it led to humiliation, insult, betrayal, rejection, and whatever else! **Romans 13:8** tells us to *"Owe no one anything except to love one another, for he who loves another has fulfilled the law."* We have to put on LOVE as a garment; we need to wear LOVE as it says in **Colossians 3:14:** *"But above all these things put on love, which is the bond of perfection."* We cannot call ourselves worshippers if we don't love."

2. Faith
The Free Dictionary defines faith as: *1. Confident belief in the truth, value, or trustworthiness of a person, idea, or thing. 2. Belief that does not rest on logical proof or material evidence; strong or unshakeable belief in something, especially without proof or evidence.* Synonyms are: *belief, trust.* I like the second definition more because it aligns with the biblical definition of faith as outlined in **Hebrews 11:1.** *"Now faith is the substance of things hoped for, the evidence of things not seen."* The Amplified Bible expands it further, *"Now faith is the assurance (the confirmation, the title deed) of the things [we] hope for, being the proof of things [we] do not see and the conviction of their reality [faith perceiving as real fact what is not revealed to the senses]."* This is the reason we can confidently call those things that are not as though they were. Our declarations backed with faith in the Word of God have creative powers. That is why we can decree a thing, and it shall come

to pass.

A few verses further down in **Hebrews 11:6**, the Bible says, *"And without faith it is impossible to please God, because anyone who comes to Him must believe that He exists and that He rewards those who earnestly seek Him."* A true worshipper's priority is to please God, and we see here that, without faith, it is impossible to please God. The God kind of faith comes from the Word of God because **Romans 10:17** states, *"So then faith comes by hearing, and hearing by the word of God."* This clearly tells us that faith must have the Word of God as its foundation. The worshipper needs to develop their faith by getting into the Word of God and getting to know God. As worshippers, we *"walk by faith, not by sight"* **(2 Corinthians 5:7)**. Walking by faith means that the spiritual supersedes the natural. Our five physical senses are not our satellite navigators; we don't rely on them. As a matter of fact, we consciously and deliberately DISREGARD them, whilst we turn in to the inner spiritual censors for discernment, which is not based on logical reasoning or rational thinking.

Our faith in God is the victory we have to overcome the world. *"For whatever is born of God overcomes the world. And this is the victory that has overcome the world—our faith."* **(1 John 5:4)**. One whose faith is deeply rooted in God will know these three truths about Him:

1. **God cannot lie.** God has integrity. He says what He means, and He means what He says; therefore, we can take Him at His Word. It is

impossible for God to lie. His standard of right and wrong does not change. Has He spoken a word? He will bring it to pass. His Word is settled forever. **Numbers 23:19** reads, *"God is not a man, that He should lie, nor a son of man, that He should repent. Has He said, and will He not do?"*

2. **God cannot fail**. Even when we fail Him, He remains true to His Word. If we are faithless, He remains faithful; He cannot deny Himself **(2 Timothy 2:13)**. God is righteous and perfect in all His ways.

3. **God cannot make a mistake**. **Isaiah 40:8** says, *"The grass withers, the flower fades, but the word of our God stands forever."* There is purpose to everything that He says, does or allows. He is unsearchable and His wisdom is infinite. God is not like mere men. This knowledge instills confidence and assurance when we go through situations that seem impossible.

Our faith is developed when we establish an intimate relationship with God and come to know Him as outlined above. This is not to say that everyone has the same level of faith. No, we are all different, and we are all works in progress. Remember that even a 'mustard seed' sized faith can move mountains. It is okay to pray for help when we find ourselves slipping into the abyss of fear and unbelief; after all, even the disciples of Jesus Christ cried out in **Luke 17:5**, *"Lord, increase our faith!"* Our faith will be tried; our faithfulness will be tried; our walk with the Lord will be tested. The scriptures confirm to us that even when we face difficult and challenging times with the right attitude, the tests will mature us in our Christian walk. **James 1:2-4** says, *"Consider it pure joy, my brothers, whenever you face trials of many kinds, because you know that the testing of your faith develops perseverance. Perseverance must finish its work so that you may be mature and complete, not lacking anything."*

During moments of trial, our faith must be backed by actions of obedience. As worshippers, we demonstrate our faith in the Word of God by our 'walk' and our 'works' because faith without works is dead, being alone. **James 2:17** says, *"So also faith, if it does not have works (deeds and actions of obedience to back it up), by itself is destitute of power (inoperative, dead)."* I read a humorous post somewhere that stated: Christians are like tea bags; drop them in hot water, and they will manifest their true colour! Our faith, or lack of it, shows up when we are under pressure. The key question for us from this section is "How deeply rooted is our faith in the Lord?" Worship flows effortlessly from a heart that is full of faith in the Lord.

3. Obedience
John 14:15 says, *"If you love Me, keep My commandments."* I was taught that obedience is the highest form of worship. In other words, the true test of a worshipper is their level of obedience to the Word of God. And what is obedience? According to *Holman's Illustrated Bible Dictionary*, a succinct definition of biblical obedience is *to hear God's Word and act accordingly.* One of the Greek terms for

obedience implies positioning oneself under someone by submitting to their authority and command. Another Greek word for obey means *to trust*, hence the phrase 'trust & obey.'

I don't need anyone to quote scriptures for me to understand that obedience is an automatic response from me if I love and respect someone; especially when I know they have my best interest at heart. How do we show that we respect and honour someone? We take their words seriously and obey them when they tell us to do something. The more I read up on the subject of obedience, the more it struck me how important obedience is to the Father. **Deuteronomy 28** is both exciting and really scary at the same time because we read about the blessings of obedience, but on the other hand, we also see what the Father says are the consequences of disobedience.

The full extent of how deeply the Father takes obedience can be found virtually everywhere in the Bible. Consider the fall of Adam…it was LACK OF obedience (disobedience) that severed his fellowship with God. There was no separation until he disobeyed God, and then he died spiritually, for to be separated from God is spiritual death. Consider Moses; disobedience prevented him from entering the Promised Land! Consider King Saul; disobedience caused his removal as king! On the other hand, consider what the Father said about David: "*I have found David the son of Jesse, a man after My own heart, who will do all My will*" **(Acts13:22)**. In other words, I have found a man after my own heart who will OBEY Me! This is how crucial this subject is to the

Father.

As a parent of four children, the Holy Spirit sometimes uses everyday events to remind me how the Father feels when we, His children, obey Him and equally how He feels when we disobey Him. I know how I feel as a parent when my child disobeys me. I feel upset, insulted and disrespected; I feel like they are pushing the boundaries and daring me to see how much they can get away with. I, therefore, cut off all privileges; as a matter of fact, discipline follows disobedience because disobedience equals rebellion. I let them know that disobedience has negative consequences, just as obedience has its rewards. On the other hand, I also know how pleasing it feels when my child is obedient! Well, this is exactly the same principle with our heavenly Father. A worshipper lives a life of obedience. That is not to say that we do not make mistakes and sometimes fail God. Living a life of obedience does not mean we are perfect, for none is perfect except the Lord; we all stumble and sometimes fall, but the most important thing is to quickly repent and get back on track. God is merciful and will forgive us when we ask for forgiveness. He is a gracious Father; His grace and mercies are new every morning!

We all know that obedience is easier 'talked' than 'walked.' It's okay to have all the head knowledge on obedience, but how do we endeavor to walk in obedience? How do we practically apply what we have learnt when we are faced with real situations in a real world? By opening our hearts and ears to the voice and the leading of the Holy Spirit, and following

His instructions. He is our Helper; there is no way we can do it by our own strength; it doesn't matter how vigilant or carefully we tread! I daresay it is impossible to walk in obedience by our own strength. It is not by power, not by might, but by the Spirit of God. We need to learn to commune and communicate with the Holy Spirit. Walking in obedience means that we will sometimes have to bite our tongues, even when we're desperate to say something. It means we will sometimes need to forgive those who have unjustly hurt us or betrayed our trust. It means we will sometimes have to give up our right to retaliate, even when it feels right to do so. It means we will sometimes have to say no to some open doors according to the leading of the Holy Spirit. It means we will sometimes have to suffer pain, even when we feel we don't deserve it. To love God is to obey God. We cannot walk in obedience by our own strength; we have to rely on the help of the Holy Spirit.

Most, if not all of us have read or heard about the Bible verse which says, "Obedience is better than sacrifice" **(1 Samuel 15:22).** The Holy Spirit opened my eyes to understand what this verse really means because this is an area in a worshipper's life where the enemy subtly and craftily creeps in to lure them into the 'self-righteous' mode. Now, let me give an analogy of what I mean. I have a son who does not like to tidy his room, so every time I tell him to tidy his room, he finds an excuse not to do it. When asked why he hasn't tidied his room, he'll come up with reasons which, in his view, justify his disobedience. He tells me how he washed the dishes, fed the rabbit, loaded the washing machine, etc. Basically he recounts all these good and noble chores he did, and then tries to claim that's enough to let him off, even though tidying his room was the one thing I asked him to do. Well, we do this with the Father as well; we pick and choose what we want to do, which areas of His Word we want to obey; we carefully avoid the areas which stretch us, and try to justify our disobedience by overcompensating in other areas that we enjoy doing. This still amounts to disobedience, which is operating in rebellion.

Obedience flows from a heart that is yielded to the Father, a life that is surrendered to do HIS will. We obey God out of our love for Him. **John 14:21** *says, "He who has My commandments and keeps them, it is he who loves Me..."* We must ask the Holy Spirit to help us in the area of obedience. A worshipper must live a life of submission and obedience to the Father for this is the love of God; that we keep His commandments! **(1 John 5:3)**.

4. Sacrifice
The Oxford Dictionaries define the word 'sacrifice' as: *1. An act of slaughtering an animal or person or surrendering a possession as an offering to a deity; 2. An act of giving up something valued for the sake of something else regarded as more important or worthy.*

The fundamental principle is that sacrifice means giving, giving up, or forfeiting something. Worship DEMANDS sacrifice. I found it really interesting that the first time the word 'worship' was used in the Bible, it was closely linked (actually SYNONYMOUS) with sacrifice. **Genesis 22** gave an account of Abraham and Isaac. Following God's request for Abraham to sacrifice his only son; whom he had waited for so long, and whom he loved so much;, Abraham chose to obey God and his obedience meant the sacrifice of his son. In **Genesis 22:5**, Abraham said to his young men, *"Stay here with the donkey; the lad and I will go yonder and **WORSHIP**, and we will come back to you."* We know what Abraham was going to do; he was going to KILL Isaac as a sacrificial offering unto God, and he termed it 'worship.'

Have you noticed that every time there was a sacrifice at the altar, there was death involved? Something died or was killed as an offering of sacrifice, and there was shedding of blood: the burnt offerings, sin offerings, thanksgiving offerings, animal sacrifices, etc. The principle has not changed; worship still requires a sacrificial 'killing' or 'dying!' Yes, Jesus Christ sacrificed His life; He paid an eternal price which exonerates us from the curse of the law; He offered the ultimate sacrifice on our behalf when He shed His blood for the remission of our sins; He became the substitutionary atonement for our sins; He redeemed and justified us by His death, so that we will not have to shed any blood on the altar anymore. Praise God for what Jesus Christ did for us. We cannot add or take away from what He has done; however, there is still a 'dying' or a 'death' of a different kind required of every worshipper: that is death to self!

In our dispensation, physical death is not required; but we need to DIE to our flesh daily, bringing our carnal needs under subjection, denying our flesh, and 'giving' or 'giving up' our will so that the Father may be glorified in us. **Romans 12:1** says, *"I beseech you therefore, brethren, by the mercies of God, that you present your bodies a living sacrifice, holy, acceptable unto God, which is your reasonable service (act of worship)."* Our daily dying and sacrifice could be the 'forfeiting' of our feelings, our finances, our resources, our time, our energy, our talents, our desires, our substance, our material possessions, our preferences, our careers, and even our friends and family members. The ultimate sacrifice is to give Him our LIFE; which is the totality of our being; spirit, soul and body! We ought to be a living sacrifice!

I know of an aspiring medical doctor who spent seven years studying medicine and just when she finally qualified, the Holy Spirit instructed her to forsake her desired career path and go into full-time ministry! I have heard many such testimonies. Sacrifice could be as simple as someone saving up money over two years to buy the car of their dreams, and when they finally do, they hear that still small voice telling them to sow that car into someone else's life, and it may be someone they don't even like! Sacrifice could mean that when others are feasting, we are fasting! It could mean that whilst others are out partying, we are in our bedrooms studying the Word or on our knees all night travailing. It could mean sowing a financial seed into a ministry when we don't seem to have enough to sort out our own problems. It could mean giving up a hobby we like or a habit we enjoy. Remember, sacrifice here is the act of offering something of value to God, or forfeiting something highly valued for the sake of God.

Having said all that, it is important to note that NOT all sacrifices are acceptable to the Father, such as the account of Cain's rejected sacrifice in **Genesis 4:3-5:** *"And in process of time it came to pass, that Cain brought of the fruit of the ground an offering unto Jehovah. And Abel, he also brought of the firstlings of his flock and of the fat thereof. And Jehovah had respect unto Abel and to his offering: but unto Cain and to his offering he had not respect. And Cain was very wroth, and his countenance fell."* Both Cain and Abel came to worship before the Lord; both bought a sacrifice. What was the difference? Why did the Father respect Abel's sacrifice, but not Cain's? I don't have all the answers, but I believe we can catch a glimpse from what **Hebrews 11:4** says: *"By faith Abel offered unto God a more excellent sacrifice than Cain, through which he had witness borne to him that he was righteous…"* The key words there being BY FAITH. The state of our heart is more important than the sacrifice itself. Whatever is not from faith is sin **(Romans 14:23)**. This is relevant and applies to every situation; whether we are bringing our tithes and offerings, sowing seeds, or fasting; the state, motive and intents of our heart are all important factors to consider. All of our sacrificial actions must prayerfully spring from our faith in God and the leading of the Holy Spirit. Worship demands sacrificial living; we can't live any which way if we want a deeper walk with the Father. There is a cost attached to true worship of the Father.

5. Prayer and Meditation

Prayer, to the Christian, is like water to a fish: INDISPENSABLE. Adam Clarke made this statement about prayer: *"A proper idea of prayer is a pouring out of the soul unto God, as a free-will offering. Prayer is the language of dependence; he who prays not, is endeavouring to live independently of God..."* A worshipper that does not pray is like a human being that cannot breathe; it's just a matter of time before his life is gone! Prayer is part and parcel of worship; the two are inseparable. Our relationship with God is only as good as our communion and communication with God, and simply put, prayer is communicating with God. Prayer may occur silently or verbally; individually or corporately, but nothing can take the place of prayer in a worshipper's life. I have yet to meet anyone who does not have seasons or periods of time when they do not struggle to create time for prayer, so you're not the only one! However, we can depend on the help of the Holy Spirit to establish a consistent prayer life.

A lot of people also complain about not knowing how to pray. The simple truth is that we learn to pray by praying. It's like physical exercise. When you start working out in the gym; it requires time, discipline and tenacity to carry on after the first few times. Although you're not immediately seeing the impact of the workout, something is happening within your body that is causing a change on the inside. The first few days are followed by excruciating body pains, and it's really easy to give up due to the temporary discomfort and inconvenience of it all. That's a time when you are the most vulnerable! But if you push through that threshold and press on courageously, you will gradually begin to see changes in the physical. Exercise actually becomes enjoyable, and you will actually miss workouts when you can't manage to get to the gym. I remember when I first registered to study at New Life Bible College in Wembley, London. My first month was a real struggle because, although we were in class at 7:00pm; the class started with praise, worship, and then prayers for about an hour and a half. Now, I was not used to praying for that long, so it was boring for me. I purposely used to arrive at 8:00pm just to join the last few minutes before lessons. That was until the Holy Spirit rebuked me! I struggled, but I had to discipline myself to get there on time. After a while, I began to actually enjoy praying; not only in class, but in my own private time. Even my husband noticed my new love for praying because our daily 6:00am prayers were becoming more and more extended. Our faith, our relationship and communion with the Lord are all strengthened through spending time with Him in prayer and meditation. Prayer requires discipline and tenacity, and requires us to create some quiet time to spend in His Word and in His presence.

For me, during periods of struggle, I get into the act of praying by spending short periods (like five minutes) in prayer at any one time, and five minutes soon turn to ten minutes, and so on. There will always be people who cannot pray for hours at a time; I am one of those people! Prayer is not only when you are locked up in a closet; prayers can take place anywhere, anytime. You can make little adjustments that can enhance your prayer life; for example, I found out I can pray longer when I have some worship music or instrumentals in the background. The simple acts soon become habits, and the habits soon become a lifestyle. Prayer enhances our worship life and draws us closer to the Father in a deep way. It is important to tarry in God's presence. He not only wants us to talk to Him, He also wants us to listen and hear Him. He is constantly speaking, if we care to be still and listen. In a fast-paced world where silence is perceived to be a waste of time, it is extremely hard to be still. I find it extremely challenging sometimes to tune out the noise. The great thing about having a relationship with the Father is that the more we get to know Him, the more we yearn to know Him more. That is certainly my personal experience.

The importance of taking time out to spend with the Lord cannot be over-emphasized, as there is a dimension of knowing that cannot be attained without spending quality time with the Holy Spirit. More than twenty years has passed since I lost my mother, but I still vividly remember what her voice sounded like; I still remember the things she taught me, told me, and shared with me. Why is that? Because we shared a very close relationship! We talked all the time; I listened to her wise counsel countless times during my growing-up years. If she called me and I picked up the phone, I didn't need to second guess who it was. In fact, just by breathing down the phone, I instinctively knew who it was! Even as a mother; although my girls sound alike and my boys sound alike, I know exactly who is speaking to me without seeing them speak. I know the distinctive differences because I have heard those voices so many times and vice versa. I can spot my child from a crowd of a thousand and vice versa. I am sure every mother can testify to this. If a mother was blindfolded in a room full of babies, she would recognize the cry of her baby amongst all the other voices. That is the level of intimacy and knowing that comes from an intimate relationship; it cannot be achieved from a distance.

John 10 talks a lot about the relationship between the sheep and the Shepherd; the importance of 'knowing.' In **John 10:27**, Jesus says, *"My sheep hear My voice, and I know them, and they follow Me."* If we back up to verse 14, Jesus says, *"I am the good shepherd; and I know My sheep, and am known by My own."* The real trap we sometimes seem to fall into as ministers is that we get so busy telling everybody else about the Lord that we forget that we need to talk to the Lord ourselves. We need to communicate with Him, spend quality time with Him, study His Word and listen to Him in order to nurture our relationship with Him. We oftentimes surround ourselves with so many activities that we hardly spend any time with Him, as demonstrated in the story of Mary and Martha in **Luke 10**. Martha was distracted with much serving whilst Mary sat at the feet of Jesus to learn and spend quality time. Jesus counseled Martha in verse 42, and told her that Mary had *"chosen what is better, and it will not be taken away from her."* The challenge is to find a balance; there is no way we can be effective channels or vessels if we do not get refilled and re-energised. Just like cars need refueling every now and then, we need time away with the Father for recharging. As they say, a prayerless life is a powerless life. That is literally a true statement.

As worshippers and worship leaders, there is no substitute for our ability to hear God, to distinguish His voice from every other voice, including our own voices and the voice of the enemy. This requires us to invest some time in 'bonding' with the Holy Spirit. As we spend quality time with Him, we take on His character; we get to familiarize ourselves with His voice and His ways. We renew our mind as we study and meditate on God's Word and worship Him **(Romans 12:2)**. Part of prayer and meditation is consecration, which simply means 'set apart.' There must be a separation from the ways and culture of the world. This means; to some people, you will be considered a geek or a nerd, but being called those names should not bother you if you see the bigger picture. There are places you can't go and there are things you simply won't do because of the God-consciousness in you. I don't mean being arrogant and snobbish. Sometimes, you take time out to fast and pray; you deny yourself of things that would otherwise draw your attention away from God.

We must feed our faith with daily bread from God's Word and spend time in prayer. A journey of a thousand miles begins with one step. If you're not sure how to pray, ask the Holy Spirit to help you! The first disciples asked Jesus, *"Lord teach us how to pray"* **(Luke 11:1)**, so it is perfectly okay to ask the Holy Spirit to help us. The Lord Jesus gave His disciples a pattern for praying in **Matthew 6** (The Lord's prayer). Our prayer time should include praying in tongues, praying in the spirit, and pushing past the soulish realm into the secret place. **1Thessalonians 5:17** tells us to *"Pray without ceasing."* The benefits of having a prayer life can never be too much; not only can it transform our personal lives, it can impact nations as seen **in 2 Chronicles 7:14:** *"If My people who are called by My name will humble themselves, and pray and seek My face, and turn from their wicked ways, then I will hear from heaven, and will forgive their sin and heal their land."* We must *continue earnestly in prayer, being vigilant in it with thanksgiving* **(Colossians 4:2)** knowing that *"The effective, fervent prayer of a righteous man avails much"* **(James 5:16)**. One who desires to be a worshipper after the Father's heart has to live a prayerful life.

6. Service

I personally think that service is probably the most underrated and undervalued aspect of worship. We are sometimes so caught up in a worldly culture of super-stardom mindset and celebrity mentality that we sometimes view service as those mundane activities reserved for the unordained congregants (i.e. those without prestigious titles). We have allowed the world's system to permeate the Kingdom to the point where we seem to have lost sight of the principles that the Lord Jesus Christ taught His disciples. We have a sense of entitlement to be served by others because of our exalted titles, so we conveniently separate service from worship. We seem to have lost sight of the profound truth that whether we are cleaning the church's toilets, sweeping the church's hall, or helping out in Sunday School; whether we are visiting those in prisons or hospitals, praying for the sick on the roadside, or feeding and clothing the homeless family on the streets, we are worshipping God. Whether we are babysitting for a neighbor, paying someone's bill, or adopting an orphan; we are worshipping God simply by availing ourselves to be of service to others.

As a starting point, I looked up the meaning of service and came up with the following general definitions from various online dictionaries. The Free Dictionary gave the following definitions:
a. Active devotion to God, as through good works or prayer.
b. An act of assistance or benefit; a favor.
c. Contribution to the welfare of others.

Other definitions were: *to act as a servant; to render assistance; to help; to answer the purpose; to be useful or of service to; to render active service, homage, or obedience to (God, a sovereign, commander, etc.) or to be used by; as of a utility.* These are all general definitions of service, but as I dug further into the Word of God, I could not help but notice that "worship" and "service," are translated from the same Greek verb, *latreuo*. The words 'serve' and 'service' were often interchangeably used with 'worship.' Various Bible versions used the words almost as synonyms. For example, Paul exhorts believers in **Romans 12:1** to be living sacrifices, which is our "reasonable service" (KJV); a "spiritual act of worship" (NIV). I, therefore, came to the conclusion that "worship" and "service" are intricately linked. What that says to me then is that you cannot call yourself a worshipper if you are not serving. Worship and service are about giving, obedience and submission. Service is ministering, and we can't be ministers if we are not ministering!

I found the account of the Disciples childishly bickering amongst themselves in **Mark 9** and **Luke 9** amusing; they were arguing about who was the greatest amongst them. I found it somewhat comical because they were a group of grown men on an ego trip! They had just been given a commission; an important assignment to go and serve the Lord through serving others, and on the way, they took their eyes off their assignment and started engaging in a frivolous power struggle. Not too dissimilar from what we currently experience in ministry today. This is happening in local churches amongst pastors, amongst music ministers, and across every aspect of ministry: that foul, divisive spirit has infiltrated the Body and is tearing relationships apart, wreaking havoc amongst the sheep; all the while, souls are crying out for ministry. Most people look down on the concept of 'servanthood,' but scramble for 'the high calling' (which is generally seen as an exalted position of power, authority and influence). Nevertheless, we know that our Lord Jesus Christ placed a very high value on servanthood and a lifestyle of service. In **Matthew 20:28** and **Mark 10:45**, He said of Himself, *"For even the Son of Man did not come to be served, but to serve, and to give His life a ransom for many."*

Every worshipper must pray for and desire a shepherd's heart; a heart for souls (people). Our Lord Jesus Christ said in **Matthew 20:26-27** and **Mark 10:43-44** *"...but whoever desires to become great* *among you, let him be your servant. And whoever of you desires to be first shall be slave of all."* Again in **Matthew 23:11,** *"But he who is greatest among you shall be your servant."* The foundation of service is love, and service is expressed in deeds more than in words. To serve is to give of what we have been given; to bless the Lord and others out of the blessings we have received, in love and out of obedience. We give of our time, money, talents, or other resources in order to serve. No matter what we see others doing, we must resolve in our hearts as Joshua did, and say as he did in **Joshua 24:15:** *"As for me and my house, we will serve the Lord".*

Service requires humility and selflessness, not position or title. In Kingdom mentality, no job or task should be beneath us if we follow the example of Jesus Christ, the Author and Finisher of our Faith. **John 13:12-15** gives an account as an example to us: *"So when He had washed their feet, taken His garments, and sat down again, He said to them, "Do you know what I have done to you? You call Me Teacher and Lord, and you say well, for so I am. If I then, your Lord and Teacher, have washed your feet, you also ought to wash one another's feet. For I have given you an example that you should do as I have done to you."* Serving, whilst inclusive of what is done in church, is not exclusive to a church building or congregational service. Ministry is service and a minister is **one who serves,** both in and out of the church. Worship involves physical expression and demonstration through service; it involves active participation in the things of God, not a passive observation by spectators. We should *"...serve the*

Lord with gladness" as **Psalm 100:2** says, and *"…
through love serve one another,"* as **Galatians 5:13**
says.

Service is summed up in **1 Peter 4:9-11** (the Amplified
Version): *"Practice hospitality to one another (those of
the household of faith). [Be hospitable, be a lover of
strangers, with brotherly affection for the unknown
guests, the foreigners, the poor, and all others who
come your way who are of Christ's body.] And [in
each instance] do it ungrudgingly (cordially and
graciously, without complaining but as representing
Him). As each of you has received a gift (a particular
spiritual talent, a gracious divine endowment), employ
it for one another as [befits] good trustees of God's
many-sided grace [faithful stewards of the extremely
diverse powers and gifts granted to Christians by
unmerited favor]. Whoever speaks, [let him do it as
one who utters] oracles of God; whoever renders
service, [let him do it] as with the strength which God
furnishes abundantly, so that in all things God may be
glorified through Jesus Christ (the Messiah). To Him
be the glory and dominion forever and ever (through
endless ages). Amen (so be it)."*

7. Humility
I love C. S. Lewis's quotes! One of them reads,
*"Humility is not thinking less of yourself; it's thinking of
yourself less."* This subject could quite easily be
another book by itself. Scripture stresses the
importance of humility so much that it is really difficult
to contain it in this short section. I looked up the
definition of humility and came up with the following
from the Free Dictionary: *the quality or state of being*

humble; modest opinion of one's own importance or rank; meekness; freedom from pride and arrogance; lowliness of mind; a modest estimate of one's own worth; a sense of one's own unworthiness through imperfection and sinfulness; the quality of being modest and respectful; egolessness; self-abasement; humbleness; an act of submission or courtesy; grounded or low. Synonyms include *modesty, meekness, humbleness; lowliness and submission.* Jesus Christ, during His time on earth, was an epitome of humility. He was clothed with the garment of humility throughout His ministry here on earth. The true meaning of humility calls for us to be like Christ and humble ourselves to serve the Lord and others. The Bible has so much to say on humility that I almost feel there is nothing to expand on as the verses are so self-explanatory; therefore, I decided to lists some of the Bible verses on humility (or lack of it)!

Matthew 18:4- *"Therefore whoever humbles himself as this little child is the greatest in the kingdom of heaven."*
Matthew 23:12- *"And whoever exalts himself will be humbled, and he who humbles himself will be exalted."*
Luke 14:11- *"For whoever exalts himself will be humbled, and he who humbles himself will be exalted."*
Luke 18:14- *"...for everyone who exalts himself will be humbled, and he who humbles himself will be exalted."*
James 4:6- *"...God resists the proud, but gives grace to the humble."*
James 4:10- *"Humble yourselves in the sight of the*

Lord, and He shall lift you up."
1 Peter 5:5- *"Likewise you younger people, submit yourselves to your elders. Yes, all of you be submissive to one another, and be clothed with humility, for "God resists the proud, but gives grace to the humble."*
1 Peter 5:6- *"Humble yourselves therefore under the mighty hand of God, that he may exalt you in due time."*
Proverbs 11:2- *"When pride comes, then comes shame; but with the humble is wisdom."*
Proverbs 22:4- *"By humility and the fear of the Lord are riches and honour and life."*

Humility is fundamental to true worship. Throughout the entire bible, the primary Hebrew and Greek words for worship mean humility. Humility means to lower one's self and submit one's self to the will of another. So when we worship, we come under submission and surrender to the Holy Spirit; allowing Him to work in and through us. Humility is always thinking of others the way Christ sees them. This is one of the hardest battles we have to fight if we are to remain usable by the Holy Spirit. I have often wondered why, in some churches, the distinguished guest ministers are asked to be in the posh waiting areas until praise and worship is finished. After praise and worship, they are ushered into the sanctuary as if they are too important to partake of the worship session. I have also been in services where the worship leader, or whomever was leading prayers, asked people to stand up or raise their hands; nevertheless, the 'big wigs' totally ignored the call whilst everyone else responds. At times like that, I wish I could be a fly on the wall of the throne room! In looking at the importance of humility in the life of a worshipper, I thought it might be helpful to look at some of the consequences of LACK of humility; therefore, I have outlined three case studies from the Bible on what happens when pride or arrogance sets in.

First, consider the account of Lucifer in **Isaiah 14:12-14:** *"How you are fallen from heaven, O Lucifer, son of the morning! How you are cut down to the ground, You who weakened the nations! For you have said in your heart: 'I will ascend into heaven, I will exalt my throne above the stars of God; I will also sit on the mount of the congregation. On the farthest sides of the north; I will ascend above the heights of the clouds, I will be like the Most High."* Remember, this was the 'choir leader' of the heavenly hosts; he wielded power, authority and influence; but he let it get to his head, which resulted in his total destruction.

Next, consider the account of King Nebuchadnezzar in the Book of Daniel, whom God had blessed and increased abundantly, but his downfall came when he became prideful and proclaimed in **Daniel 4:30,** *"Is not this great Babylon, that I have built for a royal dwelling by my mighty power and for the honour of my majesty?"* He dared to claim glory, which belonged to God to himself, and alas; he felt the full wrath of God! The account goes on to tell us that whilst the word was still in his mouth, the judgement of God came upon him instantly! The kingdom was taken away from him immediately! The king repented and with his own mouth confessed that *"those who walk in pride He is able to put down"* **(Daniel 4:37).**

Finally, consider the account of King Uzziah in **2 Chronicles 26.** He became king at 16-years-old, and the Lord prospered him greatly because he sought the Lord diligently. Verse five says, *"As long as he sought the Lord, the Lord gave him success."* After he became successful, he became arrogant and lost respect for the sanctity of the Lord's house. Verse 16 says, *"But when he was strong his heart was lifted up, to his destruction, for he transgressed against the Lord his God..."* His arrogance (lack of humility) resulted in instant leprosy! The Bible says he was a leper until the day of his death.

From the accounts above, it is clear that humility cannot be over-emphasized. If we want to seek God genuinely, we need to steer clear of what He hates. The Bible says that God hates pride **(Proverbs 6:16-17)**. Those who God used mightily were humble people; they were people who did not come with a sense of entitlement. We need to emulate Jesus, the Author and Finisher of our faith, in every area of our lives. At this point, it is important to make a distinction between genuine humility, which is distinctly different from false humility. This is a really key issue because we ought not to deceive ourselves with outward forms of humility knowing that our hearts are far from humble. God is not impressed with 'appearances.' He looks at the heart. False humility consists of belittling or trivializing one's gifts, talents, and achievements in order to impress people. In other words, we learn to perfect the act of humility without the heart of humility. I hate to say this, but this is a very rampant issue in churches where 'eye service' is widespread. I remember someone telling me about the story of a gospel artiste who openly dismisses gospel award shows or events because, according to him, they're all worldly and unscriptural; but then he secretly nominates himself for the awards! Now, this is a classic case of false humility!

Most of us find it quite hard to draw the line between having a healthy self-image and being prideful. I work in the corporate world, and we are advised to promote our achievements in order to remain relevant. Even in ministry, we are advised to do the same. We are sometimes advised that we won't gain the respect and recognition we rightly deserve unless we promote ourselves, take center stage, and claim all the credit for our successes; sometimes at the expense of others. I remember having a 360 degree assessment (a leadership exercise) at my secular workplace, and one of the statements I had to agree or disagree with was: "I feel in control of my future." I selected 'disagree' and the final report interpreted that to mean I lacked self-confidence and vision. Consequently, I had to have a follow-up meeting with the consultants to explore my reasons for 'lacking confidence.' I explained my answer from a scriptural perspective. I don't need to tell you the rest; let's just say they labeled me something or the other!

I will close this section by looking at the account in **Luke 14:7-11** when Jesus was addressing the Pharisees and lawyers.
"Now he told a parable to those who were invited, when he noticed how they chose the places of honour, saying to them, "When you are invited by

someone to a wedding feast, do not sit down in a place of honour, lest someone more distinguished than you be invited by him, and he who invited you both will come and say to you, 'Give your place to this person,' and then you will begin with shame to take the lowest place. But when you are invited, go and sit in the lowest place, so that when your host comes he may say to you, 'Friend, move up higher.' Then you will be honoured in the presence of all who sit at table with you. For everyone who exalts himself will be humbled, and he who humbles himself will be exalted."

This story basically says, be humble or risk embarrassment and disgrace! Jesus was, in effect, saying that it is better not to overestimate one's importance, as this could put one at risk of public disgrace. In conclusion, do as **Philippians 2:5-11** says, *"Let this mind be in you which was also in Christ Jesus, who, being in the form of God, did not consider it robbery to be equal with God, but made Himself of no reputation, taking the form of a bondservant, and coming in the likeness of men. And being found in appearance as a man, He humbled Himself and became obedient to the point of death, even the death of the cross. Therefore God also has highly exalted Him and given Him the name which is above every name, that at the name of Jesus every knee should bow, of those in heaven, and of those on earth, and of those under the earth, and that every tongue should confess that Jesus Christ is Lord, to the glory of God the Father."* A worshipper ought to be clothed in genuine humility.

8. Fruit of the Spirit

As I round up this chapter on the lifestyle of a worshipper, I believe with all my heart that the Lord wants me to talk about the Fruit of the Spirit, which is not really separate from points 1-7 above. More than anything, I believe this section reinforces everything that has been touched on before now. As **Matthew 7:15** says, *"By their fruits you shall know them."* So, **What is a Fruit?**

Fruit is generally defined, according to Webster's Dictionary, as *something that is birthed or borne of a seed; a produce; a product; a result; a consequence or outgrowth of something; a crop; a harvest; an offspring; something that is brought forth.* In other words, when a seed is sown, an offspring of that seed is a 'fruit.' Bringing this in context of the lifestyle of a worshipper, we know that every believer carries the indwelling presence of the Holy Spirit, so THAT presence SHOULD produce or bear fruit in our lives. The fruit of the Holy Spirit is the result of the Holy Spirit's indwelling presence in the life of a believer.

We know God made everything to produce after its own kind **(Genesis 1:11)**, so we should have something to show for having the Holy Spirit. **Galatians 5:22-23** lists nine attributes of the Fruit of the Holy Spirit: *"But the fruit of the Spirit is love, joy, peace, longsuffering, kindness, goodness, faithfulness, gentleness, self-control. Against such there is no law."* The fruit of the Holy Spirit is in direct contrast with the acts of the sinful nature in **Galatians 5:19-21:** *"Now the works of the flesh are evident, which are: adultery, fornication, uncleanness,* *lewdness, idolatry, sorcery, hatred, contentions, jealousies, outbursts of wrath, selfish ambitions, dissensions, heresies, envy, murders, drunkenness, revelries, and the like; of which I tell you beforehand, just as I also told you in time past, that those who practice such things will not inherit the kingdom of God."*

The fruit of the Holy Spirit have to do with the core of our personalities; we SHOULD develop Godly character if indeed we are in fellowship with the Holy Spirit. His personality SHOULD begin to rub off on us and begin to cause some changes to take place within and around us. When my husband and I got married, we were two poles apart in terms of personality traits; he was an extremely patient man, whilst I was an extremely impatient woman. Initially, this was a source of friction because we both moved at such different paces. He is the type that likes to take his time to think things over, consider the ins and outs, weigh the pros and cons, etc. Nevertheless; I was the impulsive, impatient and fast-paced one. If something needed doing, I wanted it done there and then; therefore, we used to get into arguments because we didn't understand one another. Now, after 25 years of being together, some of his calmness has rubbed off on me; I am a little bit more measured in my actions and decisions. That is exactly how it should work with the Holy Spirit in the worshipper's life; the fruit of the Holy Spirit should be evident in the life of a worshipper, especially the spiritually mature believer.

Every worshipper should regularly take the time out to

honestly reflect on their relationships and actions. Just like we check the oil gauge in cars, we need to check the level of our love walk; where are the proofs that we have love, joy, peace, longsuffering, kindness, goodness, faithfulness, gentleness, self-control? What are the testimonies of those we interact with on a daily or weekly basis; at home, place of work, in the community, in school, at church, in the gym, or in ministry? Do their reports tell of one who is representative of Christ? I have observed a grave error that is common in churches where 'gifts' are prioritized over 'fruit.' This error has caused untold damage to many lives and churches so it is very important that we differentiate between the fruit of the Holy Spirit and the gifts of the Holy Spirit. There is a popular saying: *"Your gift may open doors, but only character can keep them open."*

First of all, **what is a gift?** A gift is a thing given willingly to someone without payment; it is a present, something that is bestowed voluntarily and without compensation. The gifts of the Holy Spirit are endowments given by the Holy Spirit. They are grace-gifts of the Holy Spirit as a result of the infilling of the Holy Spirit; an example is the event that took place in **Acts 2:4** when the Holy Spirit filled the apostles, and they began to speak with other tongues, as the Spirit gave them utterance. The Gifts of the Holy Spirit are for service, manifested through individual believers as the Spirit of God wills. The purpose of the spiritual gifts is to edify (build up), exhort (encourage), and comfort the church. **1 Corinthians 12:4-11** outlines nine Gifts as follows:

-Three revelation (revealing) gifts—spiritual gifts that reveal something: The word of wisdom; the word of knowledge; the discerning of spirits
-Three power (doing) gifts—spiritual gifts that do something: The gift of faith; the working of miracles; the gifts of healings
-Three utterance or inspirational (saying) gifts— spiritual gifts that say something: Prophecy; different kinds of tongues; interpretation of tongues

The difficulty is that we sometimes assume that because someone has the gift, they must also have the fruit. This is not always true because the gifts are for supernatural manifestations given for edification of the Body, but the fruit is for character building and development. Fruit is developed as a result of spiritual maturity, whilst the gifts are given as the Holy Spirit wills. Remember that fruit is a product of growth, whilst gifts are bestowed as the Spirit wills. The error lies in chasing after the gifts, whilst ignoring the fruit, sometimes with devastating results. Our fruit will always give an indication of our spiritual state, so every worshipper must strive to produce 'good' fruit.

As **Philippians 4:8** says, *"Finally, brethren, whatever things are true, whatever things are noble, whatever things are just, whatever things are pure, whatever things are lovely, whatever things are of good report, if there is any virtue and if there is anything praiseworthy—meditate on these things."* And as **Matthew 5:16** says, *"Let your light so shine before men, that they may see your good works and glorify your Father in heaven."* God's ultimate goal for our lives on earth is not comfort, but character development.

PRAYER

Father, in the name of Jesus Christ, I present myself to You today in total submission and in humility. I ask that You help me to look deep within and deal with any issues that are hindering my walk with You. Create in me a clean heart, O Lord, and renew the right spirit within me. Open my eyes to see the areas that I need to change and give me the strength of character and courage to make the changes needed. I am desperate for a closer, more intimate relationship with You, and I am willing to trust and obey You with the help of Your Holy Spirit. Lord, I want to be more like You; I want to think like You, talk like You and walk like You. I want to represent You wholeheartedly, and I realize that I am not strong enough, wise enough or good enough to do this on my own. I need You every step of the way. Help me to develop godly character and to have a servant's heart in all that I do. I pray for the fruit of the Holy Spirit: love, joy, peace, patience, kindness, goodness, faithfulness, gentleness, and self-control. I thank You now for answered prayers in Jesus name. Amen.

LOST WITHOUT YOU
©Isabella Ogo-Uzodike (2009)

Verse 1
Without You, I'm just an empty vessel
Without You, I'm just a sounding brass
Without You, I'm just a clanging cymbal
Without You, there is no me

Chorus
I can't live without You
I can't breathe without You
I need You more than words can ever say
I won't exist without You
I can't survive without You
I need You more than minds will ever know
Like an eagle with no wings
I'm hopelessly lost without You

Verse 2
Without You, my being has no purpose
Without You, my song is just a noise
Without You, my mission is so pointless
Without You, there is no me

Bridge
You're the wind beneath my wings
The tower of my strength

The fountain of my peace
The centre of my joy
(Repeat)

Chapter Five: David; The Worshipper After The Father's Heart

Acts 13:22- *"And when He had removed him, He raised up for them David as king, to whom also He gave testimony and said, 'I have found David the son of Jesse, a man after My own heart, who will do all My will."*

David was the youngest of the eight sons of Jesse, and great-grandson of Boaz and Ruth **(Ruth 4:17)**. Of all the interesting characters in the Bible, David is the one person that REALLY fascinates me the most. Not because of his pure ingenuity in penning some of the most mesmerising and intriguing psalms; not because of his complex personality; not because of his notoriety; not even because of all the great feats he achieved, but because of all the men mentioned in the Bible, David is the only one the Father called "a man after My own heart" **(1 Samuel 13:14, Acts 13:22)**. Wow; what did David do to earn him such an honour?! What did he do that caught and engaged the Father's attention to such a degree? What was it about this man, who carried out some of the most atrocious acts of all the kings of Israel; who appeared to have multiple personality disorder, and who definitely was anything but perfect? What was it about

David that captivated the Father's heart? Surely, there must be lessons for us to learn from his life. In the midst of all the drama surrounding him, he must have done something right!

I so desperately want to know because I so desperately want to capture the Father's heart. I crave His attention so much that I made it my business to dig deeper into this rather intriguing character known as David to see what I could learn from his life. I wanted to get into his mind, his soul, his thinking, and his heart because I so want to be 'David' in the Father's eyes! I wanted to gain an insight into the conditions and circumstances surrounding David's life, why he wrote such profound masterpieces called the Psalms, what made him tick, and what evoked such deep emotions he so imaginatively captured in his writings? I want to feel his heartbeat, to feel the emotions which led to some of those emotional outbursts which are indelibly etched into the sands of time; I want to be the 'woman after God's own heart.'

I dug into the details of this character named David, and I found the story of a man whose life was filled with dreadful stories of jealousy, controversies, hatred, betrayal, rape, incest, murders, adultery, lust, violence, tragedies, untimely deaths, wars, assassination attempts, isolation, deceit, enmity, exile, dissensions, malice, etc. You name it; I found it in David's life! How could this be the man after the Father's heart despite his life being so full of drama and so many character flaws? What was it about this man who seemed to be a magnet for trouble and who had so many enemies? What attracted the Father to David and what attracted David to the Father?

On the other hand, I got really excited because while digging deeper into the life of David, I found David to be a passionate man whose obvious love for the Lord was to the point of obsession. He was a compassionate man with a profound reverential fear of the Lord; who constantly inquired of the Lord for direction and guidance before making decisions; who was humble and quick to repent, and most importantly; who consistently obeyed the voice of the Lord. I found a bold, courageous warrior whose trust in the Lord was unshakable; whose confidence was not in his own ability, but in the power of his God. I found a man who boldly made his boast in the Lord, and whose strength was in his God; a skilled and acclaimed musician whose anointing was potent enough to drive out an evil spirit. I found an audacious risk-taker who stepped forward to defend the name and people of the Lord when others retreated in sheer terror; a man whose fervent love for the Lord bordered on fanaticism. I found a man who was not too cool to offer undignified praise to the Lord, and did not care what others thought of his outlandish praise antics, even in the midst of ridicule. I found a man who was emotionally charged; obsessively passionate and unapologetically over-zealous about God and the things of God, even during his lowest points. I found a man whose HEART attracted and held the attention of the Master.

It literally blew my mind when I read what God said of David in **Psalm 89:19-29:**

"...I have given help to one who is mighty; I have exalted one chosen from the people. I have found My servant David; With My holy oil I have anointed him, With whom My hand shall be established; Also My arm shall strengthen him. The enemy shall not outwit him, Nor the son of wickedness afflict him. I will beat down his foes before his face, And plague those who hate him. "But My faithfulness and My mercy shall be with him, And in My name his horn shall be exalted. Also I will set his hand over the sea, And his right hand over the rivers. He shall cry to Me, 'You are my Father, My God, and the rock of my salvation.' Also I will make him My firstborn, The highest of the kings of the earth. My mercy I will keep for him forever, And My covenant shall stand firm with him. His seed also I will make to endure forever, And his throne as the days of heaven."

Wow, what an awesome privilege of favour! I could easily write a whole book on David; and I probably will one day, but for now, I will list below the key lessons I believe all worshippers should learn from David's life. His life was by no means a simple or rosy life, but he must have done something right to have captured God's attention in such a profound way.

1. **David loved God deeply and passionately**. He spent quality time in God's presence, and pro-actively sought after God with all his heart, as evidenced by his writings. He put a priority on developing his relationship with God, and he demonstrated his love for the Lord by prioritising the things of God and openly professing his love for the Lord. He gave

generously of his time and substance for the work of the Lord.

Psalm 18:1- *"I will love You, O Lord, my strength."*
Psalm 26:5- *"Lord, I have loved the habitation of Your house, and the place where Your glory dwells."*
Psalm 116:1- *"I love the Lord, because He has heard My voice and my supplications."*
Psalm 132:1-5- *"He swore an oath to the Lord and made a vow to the Mighty One of Jacob: "I will not enter my house or go to my bed-I will allow no sleep to my eyes, no slumber to my eyelids, till I find a place for the Lord, a dwelling for the Mighty One of Jacob."*

2. **David constantly inquired of the Lord before making decisions**. In other words, he always sought counsel and guidance from the Lord on what to do, and was attentive and receptive to carry out the Lord's instructions. He regularly communed and communicated with God, and constantly sought God's will for his life.

I Samuel 23:2- *"David inquired of the Lord, 'Shall I go and attack these Philistines?"*
I Samuel 30:8- *"David inquired of the Lord, 'Shall I pursue after this band? Shall I over take them?"*
2 Samuel 2:1- *"After this David inquired of the Lord, "Shall I go up into any of the cities of Judah?"*
Psalm 27:4- *"One thing I have desired of the Lord, That will I seek: That I may dwell in the house of the Lord All the days of my life, To behold the beauty of the Lord, And to inquire in His temple."*

3. **David was clothed with humility**. He had a humble and contrite heart, and was not too proud to readily admit his transgressions. Whenever he sinned, he was quick to repent and ask for forgiveness. He was open to sound counsel, rebuke and correction, even as a king.

2 Samuel 12:13- *"David said to Nathan, 'I have sinned against the LORD..."*
2 Samuel 24:10- *"I have sinned greatly in what I have done. Now, LORD, I beg you, take away the guilt of your servant. I have done a very foolish thing."*
Psalm 6:2- *"Have mercy on me, O Lord, for I am weak; O Lord, heal me, for my bones are troubled."*
Psalm 51:1-2- *"Have mercy on me, O God, according to your steadfast love; according to your abundant mercy blot out my transgressions. Wash me thoroughly from my iniquity, and cleanse me from my sin!"*

4. **David was a prayer warrior, extravagant worshipper and a zealous *praiser*.** He put priority on praising and worshipping God, thus he showed that he was more interested in pleasing God than in impressing people. He was in constant communion with God and immersed himself in prayers of repentance, consecration, thanksgiving, supplication, petition, intercession, etc. His worship was not affected, even when his request was not granted (e.g. when he lost his child with Bathsheba).

Psalm 5: 3- *"My voice You shall hear in the morning, O Lord; In the morning I will direct it to You, And I will look up."*

Psalm 55: 7- *"Evening and morning and at noon I will pray, and cry aloud, and He shall hear my voice."*

Psalm 9: 1-2- *"I will praise You, O Lord, with my whole heart; I will tell of all Your marvellous works. I will be glad and rejoice in You; I will sing praise to Your name, O Most High."*

2 Samuel 6:22- *"And I will be even more undignified than this, and will be humble in my own sight..."*

Psalm 63:3-4- *"Because Your lovingkindness is better than life, my lips shall praise You. Thus I will bless You while I live; I will lift up my hands in Your name."*

5. **David respected God ordained authority.**
   Even when he had good reason to, he refused to touch the Lord's anointed because of his reverential fear of the Lord. He was afforded multiple opportunities to effortlessly kill Saul knowing that Saul was after his life, but He reverenced God too much to touch the king. He showed great integrity.

I Samuel 24:10- *"Lo, this day your eyes have seen how the Lord gave you today into my hand in the cave; and some bade me kill you, but I spared you. I said, 'I will not put forth my hand against my lord; for he is the Lord's anointed."*

I Samuel 26:23-24- *"The Lord rewards every man for his righteousness and his faithfulness; for the Lord gave you into my hand today, and I would not put forth my hand against the Lord's anointed. Behold, as* *your life was precious this day in my sight, so may my life be precious in the sight of the Lord..."*

6. **David consistently obeyed the Lord.** His heart of obedience sprang from his profound love of the Lord and made him the man after God's heart. He often inquired of the Lord, and once he received instruction from the Lord; he obeyed the voice of the Lord. Of course, he had his moments, but he was quick to turn back to God every time he missed it.

1 Kings 11:4- *"As Solomon grew old, his wives turned his heart after other gods, and his heart was not fully devoted to the LORD his God, as the heart of David his father had been."*
1 King 15:5- *" Because David did what was right in the eyes of the Lord, and had not turned aside from anything that He commanded him all the days of his life, except in the matter of Uriah the Hittite."*
Psalm 18: 21- *"For I have kept the ways of the Lord, And have not wickedly departed from my God."*

7. **David loved the law of the Lord.** He was committed and devoted to observing the law of the Lord because he loved the Lord and knew that His Word was the truth. His delight was in the law of the Lord, and he meditated upon it with great zest and devotion.

Psalm 40:5- *"I delight to do Your will, O my God, And Your law is within my heart."*

Psalm 19:7- *"The law of the Lord is perfect, converting the soul; The testimony of the Lord is sure, making wise the simple; The statutes of the Lord are right, rejoicing the heart; The commandment of the Lord is pure, enlightening the eyes; The fear of the Lord is clean, enduring forever; The judgments of the Lord are true and righteous altogether."*
Psalm 33:4- *"For the word of the Lord is right, and all His work is done in truth.*
Psalm 119:47-48- *"And I will delight myself in Your commandments which I love. My hands also I will lift up to Your commandments, which I love, and I will meditate on Your statutes."*

8. **David had great faith in God.** Throughout his life, his faith would be tested on a grand scale, but his faith and trust in God did not waver. His faith in God made him bold and courageous in the face of danger and terror. In his confrontation with Goliath, we see him venture into a potentially fatal situation with such calm and confidence in the Lord.

I Samuel 17:45-47- *"You come against me with sword and spear and javelin, but I come against you in the name of the LORD Almighty, the God of the armies of Israel, whom you have defied. This day the LORD will deliver you into my hands, and I'll strike you down and cut off your head. This very day I will give the carcasses of the Philistine army to the birds and the wild animals, and the whole world will know that there is a God in Israel. All those gathered here will know that it is not by sword or spear that the LORD saves; for the battle is the LORD's, and he will*

give all of you into our hands."
Psalm 18:2-3- "*The Lord is my rock and my fortress and my deliverer; My God, my strength, in whom I will trust; My shield and the horn of my salvation, my stronghold. I will call upon the Lord, who is worthy to be praised; So shall I be saved from my enemies.*"
Psalm 7:1- "*O Lord my God, in You I put my trust...*"
Psalm 31:14- "*But as for me, I trust in You, O Lord; I say, 'You are my God.'*"
Psalm 62:1-2- "*For God alone my soul waits in silence; from him comes my salvation. He only is my rock and my salvation, my fortress; I shall not be greatly moved.*"

9. **David always acknowledged God and never took the glory for what God did**. He made his boast in God, as the Bible instructs in **1 Corinthians 1:31** and **2 Corinthians 10:17**. When he confronted Goliath, he made it clear that he was not coming by his own power or ability, but in the name of the Lord. In all his victories and accomplishments, he always gave glory to God.

Psalm 34:1-2- "*I will bless the Lord at all times; His praise shall continually be in my mouth., my soul shall make its boast in the Lord...*"
Psalm 144:9-10- "*I will sing a new song to You, O God; On a harp of ten strings I will sing praises to You, The One who gives salvation to kings, Who delivers David His servant from the deadly sword.*"
1 Samuel 17:37- "*The Lord, who delivered me from the paw of the lion and from the paw of the bear, He will deliver me from the hand of this Philistine.*"

10. **David loved the people of God.** David's love for God translated and transferred to God's people. This love drove him to put himself in harm's way to fight Goliath and defend God's people. He was merciful, compassionate, forgiving and showed acts of kindness. He risked his life and did not shy away from fighting many battles for God's people when provoked.

Psalm 28:9- "*Save Your people, and bless Your inheritance; Shepherd them also, and bear them up forever.*"
Psalm 29:11- "*The Lord will give strength to His people; the Lord will bless His people with peace.*"

These are some of the lessons we can learn from David's life, and I am sure there are many more lessons that we can learn if we take the time to study his life and the Psalms he wrote, but this gives us a glimpse into why he was considered to be a 'man after God's own heart.' If we can imitate his godly characteristics, we can be a people who are 'after God's own heart' as well! Of course, David was by no means a perfect man. He had his flaws and weaknesses, but in spite of all that, these qualities outlined above captured God's heart.

David's life encourages me greatly and should encourage each and every one of us, especially when we get into the 'victim' mindset; when we feel we are not sufficiently qualified or good enough for God's attention. Doesn't it give you hope to know that you do not need to be perfect to be a worshipper? It gave me so much hope, and I am so relieved that my past sins and even current and future mistakes will not disqualify me from partaking of God's grace. I am also greatly encouraged when I face challenges and difficulties, which do not at all compare to the magnitude of what David went through; I am confident that the same God is with me in and through it all. He is with us all; it is really up to us whether we trust Him or not. We can choose to obey Him and walk with Him, or we can choose to be rebellious and do our own thing. It really is up to us. I pray we all choose life!

PRAYER

Lord, I thank You for opening my eyes to see the qualities that matter to You through the life of David. Lord, You know all things; therefore, I know You are aware of the areas I need help with. You know my weaknesses and flaws; You know my struggles, so I come to you now to humbly ask for Your help. Help me develop the habits and character traits that are pleasing to You. Help me to please You in the way I relate to others. May they see in me those qualities that can only be attributed to Your presence in my life. I desperately want to be one after Your own heart, so I pray now as David, your servant, prayed: "Teach me Your way, O Lord; I will walk in Your truth; unite my heart to fear Your name. I will praise You, O Lord my God, with all my heart. And I will glorify Your name forevermore." I ask You Lord to walk with me every step of the way, and to uphold me with Your righteous hand. Plant me firmly in You that I may not waver in my faith; help me to be consistent in my ways. I thank and bless You for answered prayers in Jesus name. Amen.

MY SOURCE OF STRENGTH
©Isabella Ogo-Uzodike (2009)

Verse 1
When my burdens feel so heavy
And my spirit man grows weary
When my flesh feels weak
And all looks bleak
There's a name that I can call
In my sadness, He is joy
In my weakness, He is strength
In my brokenness, He is healing
In my darkness, He is light

Chorus
My source of strength is Jesus
My light of hope is Jesus
My Cornerstone is Jesus
Precious Lamb of God
My Prince of Peace is Jesus
My Bread of life is Jesus
My Righteousness is Jesus
Precious Lamb of God

Chapter Six: Why Should We Worship?

Matthew 4:10- *"Then Jesus said to him, 'Away with you, Satan! For it is written, "You shall worship the LORD your God, and Him only you shall serve."*

C S Lewis *said, "A man can no more diminish God's glory by refusing to worship Him than a lunatic can put out the sun by scribbling the word 'darkness' on the walls of his cell."* ABSOLUTELY! I remember 'accidentally' watching an episode of Simpsons (which I do NOT subscribe to in the least!), when one of the actors made a foolish, offensive and ignorant comment. He offhandedly said something like "Well, God is very powerful, but he must be very insecure." His reason for such a misguided conclusion was,"If God was not insecure, why did He require worship? It's only those on an ego-trip who would want to be worshipped," he said. Immediately after I heard that, two scriptures came to mind. First one is **Acts 17:24-25,** which states, *"God, who made the world and everything in it, since He is Lord of heaven and earth, does not dwell in temples made with hands. Nor is He worshiped with men's hands, as though He needed anything, since He gives to all life, breath, and all things."* And the second Scripture is **Psalm**

50:12, which says, *"If I were hungry, I would not tell you; For the world is Mine, and all its fullness."*

Someone might ask the question, "How are these Scriptures related to the question of whether God is egoistical or not?" My point is: God does not need ANYTHING from ANYONE to be who He already is! God is God all by Himself; He is the self-existent One; He is all sufficient; nothing missing, nothing broken! Nothing we think, say or do can add to or take away from who He is. Our opinions or perception of Him does not alter His identity; He is sovereign! He holds the power and authority to force everything and everyone to worship Him; but yet, He gave us all free will. We have the liberty to choose whether to worship Him or not.

In my personal view, asking a Christian "Why should you worship" is like asking a human being "Why should you breathe?" The ability to breathe is the difference between a living person and a dead person. If you don't breath, you die! Simply put, if I don't worship God, I am spiritually dead. Worship is to the believer what an engine is to a car. Remove the engine and everything else is worthless; it doesn't matter how aesthetically appealing it looks. Worship is an absolutely indispensable part of the Christian experience; our eternal destiny depends on the worship of the true, living and glorious God. Anything and everything done to pleasure and honour God is worship! The debates and misconceptions about worship arise when we narrow down worship to mean music, songs and singing in church services.

I recall once when one of my kids asked me a question that gave me a lot of food for thought. He asked, "Mum, will I go to hell if I don't worship God?" I had to pause to answer that one. It would have been easy to say 'yes' immediately, but I sensed the need to go deeper. It sounds like a pretty straightforward question with a simple answer, but I asked him, "So what do you do for God that you don't do for anyone else?" He paused and then said, "Well; I ask Him for things and He gives it to me." I said, "That's true; you also ask me and dad for things, and we give it to you." He responded, "Well; I praise Him," and I said, "That's true, but you also praise me; you praise your brother and your sisters; you praise your friends; you even praise celebrities you see on TV, total strangers whom you have never met; so what's so special about the praise you give to God? You have not reserved it exclusively for Him." He paused again and answered, "Oh yes; I know! I pray to Him, and I don't pray to you or anyone else!" Anyway, this dialogue went on and on, and in conclusion; I said to Him, "If you don't worship God, you don't love God; and if you don't love God, then He won't want to bring you to heaven because you'll be so miserable being in His presence and worshipping Him forever! He loves you too much to force you into such misery!" We laughed about it, but it is true. I then asked him, "Have you ever seen a fish that doesn't swim?" Of course, he answered, "no." "Well, that's because fish don't have a choice but to live in water, so if they don't know how to swim, they'll drown." End of conversation!

So, why should we worship God?

1. We worship God because we were created for God's glory

The purpose of our creation is to pleasure and glorify God. The glory of God is a golden thread that must run through all our thoughts, words and actions. **Psalm 29:2** urges every one of us to: *"Give unto the Lord the glory due unto His name; worship the Lord in the beauty of holiness."* Our worship brings Him glory and pleasure; our praise brings Him glory, and that is the purpose of creation; to glorify God.

Isaiah 43:7- *"Everyone who is called by My name, Whom I have created for My glory; I have formed him, yes, I have made him."*

Revelations 4:11- *"You are worthy, O Lord, to receive glory and honor and power: for you have created all things, and for your pleasure they are and were created."*

2. We worship God because we are chosen to proclaim God's praise

God Himself chose us to proclaim the excellences of His name on the earth and declare His wonderful works. We are the light of the world and the salt of the earth, so His praise should continually be in our mouths as David said in **Psalm 34:1**. Ours is a message of faith and hope; we are called to be atmosphere changers through our praise and worship. Our presence in any place should bring light (illumination, hope, encouragement, vision, transformation) to an otherwise gloomy and hopeless place. This is the purpose for which He called us out of darkness: to show forth His praise.

1 Peter 2:9- *"But you are a chosen generation, a royal priesthood, a holy nation, His own special people, that you may proclaim the praises of Him who called you out of darkness into His marvellous light..."*
Psalm 95:3- *"Declare His glory among the nations, His wonders among all peoples."*

3. We worship God because we are called to worship God

God has called us to worship Him; we are called to worship God because He is worthy of our worship. It was part of the very purpose of our creation. God seeks true worshippers who will worship Him in spirit and in truth. Every believer is called to be a worshipper; it is a call to focus our mind, heart, and attention on the worship of God.

Psalm 95:6-7- *"O come, let us worship and bow down; let us kneel before the Lord our maker. For he is our God; and we are the people of his pasture and the sheep of his hand..."*
Psalms 96:9- *"O worship the LORD in the beauty of holiness: fear before him, all the earth."*
Psalms 99:9- *"Exalt the LORD our God, and worship at his holy hill; for the LORD our God is holy."*

4. We worship God because we are commanded to Worship God

I remember the 'why' phases when my kids were between the ages of two and five years. They tended to question everything with a "why?" and sometimes I got so irritated that I would simply just snap, "Because I said so!" We are commanded to worship no other god but the Lord; we are also commanded to love God with all our heart, soul, mind and strength. This is the foundation of our Christian faith. In worshipping God, we are expressing our love for Him; we are offering Him that which is exclusively reserved for Him alone, and we are fulfilling that which is commanded in scripture. When something is commanded, it is an instruction, an order, and a mandate. This means we have an obligation to obey.

Exodus 34:14- *"For you shall worship no other god, for the LORD, whose name is Jealous, is a jealous God."*

Mark 12:30- *"And you shall love the Lord your God with all your heart, with all your soul, with all your mind, and with all your strength.' This is the first commandment."*

Luke 4:8 & Matthew 4:10- *"And Jesus answered and said to him, Get you behind me, Satan: for it is written, You shall worship the Lord your God, and him only shall you serve."*

5. We worship God because He is worthy and He deserves our Worship

The Lord is great and greatly to be praised (**Psalm 96:4**). We ought to worship God because of Who He is and what He has done. God so loved the world that He gave His only-Begotten Son, Who came that we may have eternal life. Even while we were yet sinners, God loved us enough to pay the ultimate price for our redemption. He truly deserves our worship.

Psalm 86:8-10- *"Among the gods there is none like You, O Lord; Nor are there any works like Your works. All nations whom You have made shall come and worship before You, O Lord, And shall glorify Your name. For You are great, and do wondrous things; You alone are God."*
Psalm 96:8- *"Give to the Lord the glory due His name; bring an offering, and come into His courts."*
Psalm 100:4-5- *"Enter into His gates with thanksgiving, And into His courts with praise. Be thankful to Him, and bless His name. For the Lord is good; His mercy is everlasting, And His truth endures to all generations."*
Revelation 4:11-*"You are worthy, O Lord, to receive glory and honor and power; for You created all things, and by Your will they exist and were created."*

6. We worship God because we love God

All of the reasons above are all compelling reasons to worship God, however, from my personal perspective; the most exciting reason to worship God is because we love Him! A worshipper delights in Him and counts it an awesome privilege to worship Him; not because they have been commanded to, but simply because they desire to worship Him. When I think of the Lord, my heart swells with affection; my heart melts in adoration; my whole being lights up, and I can't help but be in awe of Him. I can completely identify with **Isaiah 61:10**, which reads, *"I will greatly rejoice in the Lord, My soul shall be joyful in my God; For He has clothed me with the garments of salvation, He has covered me with the robe of righteousness, As a* *bridegroom decks himself with ornaments, And as a bride adorns herself with her jewels."* This love is extravagant, infectious and overwhelming. Thank You, Lord!

I close this chapter with **1 Chronicles 16:23-29:** *"Sing to the Lord, all the earth; proclaim the good news of His salvation from day to day. Declare His glory among the nations, His wonders among all peoples. For the Lord is great and greatly to be praised; He is also to be feared above all gods. For all the gods of the peoples are idols, But the Lord made the heavens. Honour and majesty are before Him; Strength and gladness are in His place. Give to the Lord, O families of the peoples, Give to the Lord glory and strength. Give to the Lord the glory due His name; Bring an offering, and come before Him. Oh, worship the Lord in the beauty of holiness!"*

PRAYER

Father, I come to You now as one who is hungry for more of You. I ask in the name of Jesus, that You draw me closer to You, and envelop me in Your arms so that I may know Your sweet presence in a higher and deeper dimension of intimacy. I yield myself: spirit, soul and body completely to You right now. Lord, touch my heart; help me to worship You without holding anything back. Please teach me how to be a true worshipper, the type of worshipper that You are seeking. Make me a delight to You; cause my worship to be as a sweet-smelling savour to You, my Lord.

Break down every wall of resistance and reservation in and around me; tear down every hindrance to my worship experience, and give me a new heart, and I new heart; a heart of worship. I love You with all my know that You are gracious, merciful and attentive to the cry of Your children, so I thank You for answered prayers in Jesus name. Amen.

PSALMIST'S CORNER ♪

MY HEART BEATS FOR YOU
©Isabella Ogo-Uzodike (2009)

Verse 1
I wanna dwell in Your presence
I wanna feast at Your table
I wanna drink from Your fountain
I wanna rest at Your feet

Chorus
My heart beats for You
My soul longs for You
My joy is full, My strength renewed
When I am here with You
(Repeat)

Verse 2
I wanna be soaked in Your fragrance
I wanna be clothe in Your glory
I wanna be filled by Your Spirit
I wanna be wrapped in Your arms

Bridge
I'll wash Your feet with my tears
I'll try them too with my hair
Anoint your feet with my oil
Bring to You my all
(Repeat)

Chapter Seven: Dispensations Of Worship

Hebrews 1:1-2- *"God, who at various times and in various ways spoke in time past to the fathers by the prophets, has in these last days spoken to us by His Son, whom He has appointed heir of all things, through whom also He made the worlds."*

Someone asked me the question, "What is the point of looking at Old Testament worship since it does not apply to us?" Whilst that is a valid question, every scripture is written for a specific purpose, and we must get a sound understanding and a wholesome perspective of the Word of God. In this case we are looking at the subject of worship. We need to dig deep into the subject because, just as there is a scriptural and acceptable way to worship God, there is also worship that is unacceptable to God in our dispensation. We need to gain sound knowledge, clear understanding and godly wisdom to worship God on His own terms. This is by no means a comprehensive theological exposition of dispensations, but I pray it helps someone gain a better insight into worship. My pastor taught me a profound truth, and this truth is always at the back of my mind when I study scripture. He said the Old Testament is the New Testament concealed, and the

New Testament is the Old Testament revealed. In essence, it is not enough to have one side of the picture; they are two sides of the same coin and were written for our learning. **Romans 15:4** says, *"For whatever things were written before were written for our learning, that we through the patience and comfort of the Scriptures might have hope."* And **2 Timothy 3:16-17** reads, *"All Scripture is given by inspiration of God, and is profitable for doctrine, for reproof, for correction, for instruction in righteousness, that the man of God may be complete, thoroughly equipped for every good work."*

So what is a dispensation? The Free Dictionary defines dispensation in theological terms to mean: *the divine ordering of worldly affairs*, and also as *a religious system or code of commands considered to have been divinely revealed or appointed.* The Oxford Dictionaries defines dispensation as *a political, religious, or social system prevailing at a particular time and specifically.* In Christian theology, a dispensation is a divinely ordained system prevailing at a particular period of history. Dr. L. S. Chafer defines dispensation as *a specific, divine economy, a commitment from God to man of a responsibility to discharge that which God has appointed him.* The Scofield Bible defines dispensation as *a period of time during which man is tested in respect to his obedience to some specific revelation of the will of God.* Dispensationalism is a method of interpreting history that divides God's work and purposes toward mankind into different periods of time.

When we talk about dispensations of worship, we are broadly looking at the ways we, the created; have related, interacted, communed and fellowshipped with God, our Creator in worship over periods of time from creation. There have been many arguments, debates and counter-arguments about how many dispensations there are based on Bible accounts, but that is not my focus, and to be honest; I am not interested in all the theological and dogmatic arguments. My objective for delving into this is to help the reader gain a deeper insight into the nature and operations of the Father, so that we may effectively engage with Him in our worship. If we desire to offer Him acceptable worship, we need to understand the acceptable way to worship Him **on His terms**.

Somebody may ask the question, "Does this mean that God changes over time?" The short answer is no; God is unchanging. As **Malachi 3:6** states, *"For I am the Lord, I do not change…"* All His attributes are eternal; the Creator exists outside of time and change; however, the **created** is subject to change. People are created; seasons are created; time is created; systems are created; laws are created, and creation was created; therefore, everything and everyone is subject to change **EXCEPT GOD IN HIS NATURE AND ESSENCE.** God is absolutely perfect in all His ways, and He is the unchanging Changer.

I sat through a teaching on worship by a Pastor last year and some of the things he highlighted left a lasting impression. He broke down the key differences between worship in the old and worship in the new dispensations by saying that the **principle** of worship remains the same; the **purpose** of worship is fundamentally the same, but the **practice** of worship has been redefined and completely changed. Breaking it down further, he explained it thus:

*Principle: (The What) - The underlying Principle of worship is to give God glory; to honour, reverence and adore Him. Whilst the old dispensation worship was in Law, the new dispensation is on Grace. In worshipping God, we acknowledge His sovereignty in relation to creation. He is the Creator Who is worshipped by His creation. Worship is completely exclusive to God. This principle has not changed. Worship is "in Him, through Him, by Him, to Him, and about Him."

*Purpose: (The Why) - The purpose of worship is to please God, to obey God and to humbly submit to His sovereignty. In **Revelation 4:11,** we read how the elders in their worship declare, *"Thou art worthy, O Lord, to receive glory and honour and power: for thou hast created all things, and for thy pleasure they are and were created."* Our purpose in life (and therefore, in worship) is to bring God pleasure. Although worship in the old dispensation was legalistic, the purpose of worship remains fundamentally unchanged. Having said all that, the old dispensation was more about man finding his way back to God (after Adam's spiritual death), whilst the new dispensation is more about God reaching down to reconcile His people back to Himself by giving us His dear Son and sending us the Holy Spirit to help us. The Father; through His Son, has created a conducive environment for reconciliation and fellowship. Worship in the era of the Law was more about appeasing God,

whilst worship in the dispensation of Grace is more about pleasing God.

*Practice: (The How/ Where/ When) - The practice of worship is really where the key differences lie between the old and the new. What pleased the Father in the old dispensation were certain types of burnt offerings, specific locations, precise times and seasons, specific buildings, etc. What pleases Him in the new dispensation is 'spirit and truth' worship with less emphasis on the outward display of ritualistic duties. Outlined below are the key differences in practice between the old and the new dispensations.

The old dispensation was the dispensation of the law. In the old dispensation, worship was a complex and intricate undertaking. If a person in Israel wanted to worship the Lord, they had to go to a specific building; the temple, which was located in a particular city; Jerusalem. He had to observe a stringent set of laws about the yearly cycle of feasts, the priesthood, the Sabbath, the calendar, etc. The rules were so strict that it included specifications on room measurements, furniture, types of sacrifices (including foods and drinks), various washings and the manner of offering them. The account can be read in **Hebrews 9**. In the old dispensation, access to God was strictly restricted to a few officials, and even then; they could only approach the Holy of Holies after rigorous preparation, and only at certain times of the year, or else they would be struck dead. This fellowship was limited; only the high priest could come once a year into God's very presence, have fellowship with Him and make atonement for the people's sins. This was the people's access to the Father through their High Priest representative.

So essentially worship, in the old dispensation, was based on LAW: ritualistic, legalistic, religious, strictly regulated, outward performances, animal sacrifices, etc.

- Objects of worship were specifically done to the type of offering, sacrifice and gifts
- The Temple at Jerusalem was the set place of worship
- The process was highly regimented
- Religious feasts and occasions were done during fixed seasons
- There were specific designated times set for worship to take place
- Worship was strictly regulated with specific ordinances
- Only particular personnel could carry out activities after stringent preparations (i.e. the Levitical Priests)
- Access was tightly restricted, and any breaking of protocol was severely punished

In looking at the new dispensation, we are blessed that we have a better covenant according to **Hebrews 8:3-6**: *"But now He has obtained a more excellent ministry, inasmuch as He is also Mediator of a better covenant, which was established on better promises."* The new dispensation is the dispensation of the Grace of God. The temple of God is no longer a building of stone and wood, but the Believer. We are no longer required to go to a certain building at a set time or certain holy days of the year to worship.

Corporate worship is still required (we should not forsake the gathering of the saints as instructed in **Hebrews 10:25**); however, the gathering could be anywhere, any time or season because we are the temple. The Word of God says that where two or three are gathered together in His name, He is in their midst. In the new dispensation of Grace, we; the redeemed, are the church; the Bride of Christ. Our acceptable worship does not have to be offered under the legalistic, ritualistic practices of old, but we ought to be a 'living sacrifice' because every day is the Lord's Day. God has made us kings and priests **(Revelation 1:6, Revelations 5:10),** and in the era of Grace, we have the privilege of experiencing freedom and spontaneity in worship under the leadership of the Holy Spirit.

- Worship in the new dispensation is based on GRACE (in spirit and in truth, freedom from ritualistic sacrifices, spiritual, heart condition, living sacrifice, etc.)
- The 'Temple' is no longer a building or house built with hands in a specific location
- We have the indwelling presence of the Holy Spirit, Who is our Helper, Comforter, and Intercessor
- Focus is on relationship and heart condition, not man-made religion
- The restrictions of worshipping during specific times, seasons or cycles have been lifted
- The burdens of animal sacrifices have been lifted as the blood of Jesus has paid the price
- Accessibility to the Father is open to everyone through the Son

- Legal burdens have been discarded; worship is no longer a regimented, highly structured exercise
- Spiritual restrictions have been abolished; we are all high priests with access to the Holy of Holies, and together we have an accessible High Priest and Advocate: Jesus Christ
- Burden of strict ordinances has been abolished; however, new dispensations ordinances have been established such as: Baptism **(Matthew 28:19-20)**, Breaking Of Bread **(Acts 2:42; 1 Corinthians 11:23-26)**, Fellowship **(Hebrews 10:24-25)**, etc.

The clearest distinction we can make between the old and the new has to come from **Hebrews 9:11-14** which says, *"But Christ came as High Priest of the good things to come, with the greater and more perfect tabernacle not made with hands, that is, not of this creation. Not with the blood of goats and calves, but with His own blood He entered the Most Holy Place once for all, having obtained eternal redemption. For if the blood of bulls and goats and the ashes of a heifer, sprinkling the unclean, sanctifies for the purifying of the flesh, how much more shall the blood of Christ, who through the eternal Spirit offered Himself without spot to God, cleanse your conscience from dead works to serve the living God?"*

Worship in the new dispensation is wrapped up in **John 4:23-24**: *"But the hour is coming, and now is, when true worshippers will worship the Father in spirit and in truth, for the Father is seeking such to worship*

Him. God is a spirit and they that worship Him must worship Him in spirit and in truth." True worship must be "in spirit," meaning that it must involve the inner man, and the heart. It is more than the mere outward displays of religious routines. Although we have been released from the limitations and rigidity of the old dispensation, the verse above clearly qualifies the type of worship the Father seeks. The word "must" makes the requirement absolute, meaning that it is not optional. Here the word "must" is expressing that in spirit and in truth is the only way to acceptably worship God.

In concluding this chapter, I feel it is really important to sound a note of warning to all of us because there is a real danger for some to trivialize the act and practice of worship due to a warped perception of the true meaning of worship in the new dispensation. It is true that we are no longer under the Law, but under Grace; we are no longer just servants because we have the privilege of sonship, but that does not take away from Who God is. God is still sovereign; the affairs of God should not be treated casually, and the presence of the King should not be taken for granted. There is a danger of the spirit of familiarity creeping in when we operate from a mindset of 'anything goes.' We must not lose our reverential fear for God under any circumstance because righteousness and justice are the foundations of His throne **(Psalm 89:14, Psalm 97:2)**.

I heard a preacher once say, "I do not ask God for things; I command Him!" Now, whilst we can justify using the word 'command' as it relates to **Isaiah 45:11**, our relationship with the Lord must be based on reverence, and our fellowship with Him must come from a heart full of humility. Grace is a gift from God, and that gift is His to give and His to take away. We should never come to Him with a sense of entitlement! **Ephesians 2:8:** *"For by grace you have been saved through faith and that not of yourselves; it is the gift of God."*

Grace affords us liberty in worship and fellowship; however, we ought to recognize that this liberty does not bring disrespect, chaos, disorderliness or the spirit of familiarity with it. Jesus Christ came to fulfill the law, not to abolish it. **Romans 8:1-4:** *"There is therefore now no condemnation to those who are in Christ Jesus, who do not walk according to the flesh, but according to the Spirit. For the law of the Spirit of life in Christ Jesus has made me free from the law of sin and death. For what the law could not do in that it was weak through the flesh, God did by sending His own Son in the likeness of sinful flesh, on account of sin: He condemned sin in the flesh, that the righteous requirement of the law might be fulfilled in us who do not walk according to the flesh but according to the Spirit."*

PRAYER

Dear Lord, I thank You for the ultimate price You paid to reconcile me back to the Father. Thank You for Your grace and mercy, which endures forever; thank You for being my High Priest and Advocate, and thank You for loving me despite my imperfections. I present myself to You as a living sacrifice and lay down my all before You in humble adoration. Lord, I ask for a fresh anointing for worship upon me; ignite in me a fire that cannot be quenched or satisfied by anything or anyone else. Help me to worship You as You require so that my worship will be pleasing and acceptable to You. Bring to my remembrance all I have learnt so far, and etch these revelations in my consciousness so that I will walk in Your ways and according to Your precepts. I open my heart to You to reveal even deeper truths to me so that I may grow in wisdom and knowledge of You. I thank You, and I bless Your Holy name forevermore in Jesus name. Amen.

I CHOOSE TO STAY
©Isabella Ogo-Uzodike (2009)

Verse 1
Of all the things that I could do or be this moment
Of all the choices I could ever make in life
Of all the places I could ever be this instant
My favourite place to be is here with You

Chorus
I choose to stay
I choose to love You
I choose to glorify and praise Your holy name
I choose to praise
I choose to worship
I choose to magnify and honour You always

Verse 2
Some choose to put their confidence in worldly
pleasures
Some choose to put their trust in chariots and horses
But we the righteous, sanctified and washed by His
Blood
Will rest our hope in Jesus Christ our King

Bridge
Before I even knew You
You chose me as Your own
You gave Your life as ransom for my soul

And now I have my free will
I choose to live for You
To give my life to You as a living sacrifice

Chapter Eight: Role Of Music In Worship

Colossians 3:16- *"Let the word of Christ dwell within you with all wisdom, teaching and admonishing one another with psalms and hymns and spiritual songs, singing with thankfulness in your hearts to God."*

I decided to dedicate a chapter in this book to speak on the role of music in worship because music is an integral part of worship. There have been so many write-ups on this subject, but most of the writings have really been about the appropriateness of style, genre, technique, order, arrangements and progression of the music used in worship. Whilst all those factors are really useful to know and can be quite vital in congregational or corporate worship, my focus is not on the outward performances, but more on the inward state of affairs. In other words, the focus is more on the unseen rather than on the seen. As stated in **2 Corinthians 4:18**, *"While we do not look at the things which are seen, but at the things which are not seen. For the things which are seen are temporary, but the things which are not seen are eternal."* There is an over-saturation of books, manuals, CDs, DVDs and other media that teaches how to work on your voice, breathing, self-confidence, stage presence and managing nerves for effective personal impact during music ministrations. Those are all needful for maximizing the effectiveness of music in worship, but like I said; they are not the focus here.

Over the years, I have come across all sorts of theological debates on the use of worship music. I was astounded to read (and I can't remember where) an article outrightly condemning the use of music in worship. They inferred that music, at best, is a distraction from worshipping God, and at worst, a substitute for true worship (insinuating that music itself had become an idol). Whilst I can appreciate the point about making sure music does not become an idol, I can find no evidence to support the mindset and theory that music takes away from true worship. My experience has certainly been that music has tremendously enhanced my worship experience. I have also read some articles that are heavily critical of certain genres of music. In fact, I have heard of certain churches who refer to 'rap' music as "the devil's music," and they look upon 'rock' music with disdain; therefore, they will not allow any such 'demonic' music to play in their gatherings.

Music is a catalyst for worship. We sometimes forget that worship is not a musical activity, but a function of the heart. Music should be used to enhance our expression of our adoration of God, thereby facilitating worship, and not as an end in itself. The focus should be on the content, not the style of the music! Music, in my view, does add a richer dimension to worship, and there are depths of expression I could never reach by just 'saying' the words I could by 'singing.' Like the rest of creation, music is designed for God's glory **(Isaiah 48:11; Romans 11:36)**. Music affects the emotional faculties, etching the Word of God into the heart and memory in a way that mere words cannot. The message in the music should convey our love for God, and reinforce scriptural teachings; not diminish or water down the Word of God to make it more palatable. Music is not synonymous with worship because many people cannot sing, but they are worshippers. In **Luke 7**, the woman who anointed Jesus' feet is exemplary as a worshipper; she was not singing or playing any musical instruments, but she was worshipping in a most profound way.

I have come to realize that it is human nature to criticize what we do not understand. Oftentimes, we base our judgment of right or wrong, good or bad, anointed or not anointed on our denomination, age, culture, customs, traditions, orientation, and level of exposure much more than the Word of God. If it is unfamiliar, our automatic response is rejection or condemnation. If what we see or hear does not line up with what we have learnt or have been taught during our formative years; in our subjective view; it must be wrong, inappropriate or unappealing to God. We play God! Someone once challenged a rapper to show them where in the Bible 'rap' music was mentioned, and the rapper, in turn, asked the enquirer to show them where exactly 'worship music' was specifically defined in scripture in terms of what it should sound like. What I am saying, in essence, is that we need to be careful to avoid making man's traditions or personal preferences take precedence over the Word of God when it comes to music in worship. In our dispensation, the Bible is not prescriptive on style and structure of worship music, but the Bible is absolutely clear on purpose and focus of worship music. The chief end is to glorify God and edify the Body, not to impress or entertain people.

To an extent, we are all guilty of being quite subjective in our choice of worship music, and that in itself is not wrong; what is wrong is closing our minds to other people's preferences and adopting an arrogant 'holier-than-thou' attitude towards those who have a different taste than ours because we imagine their style to be too carnal or too worldly for God. I personally cannot imagine worshipping or being in the spirit whilst listening to a 'rap' song. I would be too distracted trying to understand what is being rapped, but my teenage children can worship whilst listening and bopping their head to rap music. That doesn't make me spiritually superior or closer to God than they are; it just means that we have different taste in music; in this particular case, there is an element of generational influence. Whether I eulogize it, sing it, say it, shout it or whisper it to God does not affect the Father, but it does affect me, the worshipper. Jesus Christ made it clear in **John 4:23-24** what the essential or key elements of worship that pleases the Father:

1. The content of the worship (is it TRUTH based on the Word of God?)

2. The state of the heart of the one who offers the worship. (Is it SPIRIT based on a right-standing relationship with God?)

I remember a couple who, upon joining our local church, insisted that our choice of worship songs were wrong and needed to be revamped completely. They came from a background where a certain style of music was used for praise and worship, so they met the change with vehement resistance. As far as they were concerned, we were in error for not worshipping with the same type of music they were used to. Our music was not ministering to them, so they were struggling to worship with the style of music we were using in worship; it had nothing to do with the content of the worship songs; they just didn't flow with the style. Whilst this is totally understandable from a 'change management' perspective, it has no scriptural basis. We all naturally resist change and need time to adjust and adapt to change, **but** we must realize that we are not the recipients of the worship; there is only one recipient and His name is God, the Father! Worship is exclusively for Him. I totally agreed that worship leaders need to be responsive to the needs of the congregation in corporate worship to facilitate and encourage an atmosphere and attitude which is conducive for worship; however, that should not become the primary focus.

My take is: if we insist on worshipping God only through a particular style of music; that's alright, but we should remember that our musical style and preferences are not necessarily the only ones acceptable to the Father. I have to confess, I was one of those who used to regard the more boisterous music ministers as shallow noise makers who were not serious minded. For me, the real worshippers were the ones who sang slow, soulful, solemn almost melancholic sounds; those who lay on their faces and bawled their eyes out (like me); these were the true worshippers, as far as I was concerned. I have since caught a revelation that true worship is much more than music style or sound, and definitely more than the outward actions we portray! Our choice of worship music says more about our orientation and personality than about the authenticity of our worship or the suitability of the music as far as the Father is concerned. Whatever the sound or style, worship reverentially offered from a true heart; in humility, based on God's Word and led by the Holy Spirit is wholly acceptable to the Father. Scripture, not tradition should govern all things as instructed in **Mark 7:6-9**.

We could have a 'worship' gathering with the greatest ensemble, best sounding orchestra, fantastic vocalists, sophisticated cutting-edge gadgets, perfect ambience and incredible showmanship without the heart for the Lord and love for His people, and the best we can give is great entertainment! A few years ago, the Holy Spirit convicted me about this. I was part of a board which organized a massive high-profile event. The event itself was held at a prestigious location; wonderful ambience, immaculate sound, awesome vocalists and was attended by prominent crème de la crème of the UK gospel scene, but we were lacking in the area of charity and hospitality. Although the project itself was a great success in many ways, a number of ministers walked away feeling discouraged because they felt mistreated, dishonoured and unappreciated. The Holy Spirit clearly spoke to my heart through that experience, and I will never forget the deep conviction I felt in my spirit that day.

Drawing from my personal experience over the years, I have been to various churches to minister, and my experiences have been as diverse as the people in the churches. Some churches look impeccable; their pews are filled to overflowing with a perfectly dressed, cultured congregation; but in the midst of all the glamour, what hits the spirit is what is NOT present: LOVE. They have the most beautiful edifice, but you feel caged and cagey; the people are decked to their teeth in their Sunday's best, but you can't get them to smile or lift up holy hands. They serve you the most delicious-looking banquet with expensive crockery, but you're too nervous and uncomfortable to touch it! They treat you like they're doing you a huge favour by allowing you to step into the church, and you leave with a fat cheque feeling drained, lifeless and worthless. On the other hand, I have been to some old raggedy shacks with a handful of people, and have left feeling revived and refreshed by the move of the Holy Spirit. Why have I said all of this? Because the foundation of everything we do must be LOVE. The Father's heart is for His people; His concern is for His people; His love is for His people. Above the music, the sound, the appearance, the accolades, the style of music, the agenda, the programme and the creative display; He places priority on LOVE. Loving and caring for His children are aspects of the worship we offer to the Father. Loving His people is part of loving Him. Meeting the needs of His people is the bottom line.

Going back to the subject of music in worship; music is a powerful tool for both personal and corporate worship because music has a universal appeal which transcends boundaries to hit the spirit, heart and soul.

The fascinating thing about music is that we can often sing in languages we cannot speak. I have witnessed the most terrible stutterers sing so beautifully without missing a beat. Music can get across what mere words cannot; it takes the singer or musician beyond the limits of mere recitation. In my opinion, music brings words to life and helps us to effectively articulate our passionate emotions, which would otherwise sound monotonous and lifeless. Singing is really an elevated form of speech. In other words, music makes it possible to communicate and commune with God in a richer, deeper, wider, higher and greater dimension than mere recitations of phrases. Such is the mystery and power of music. Music articulates the inexpressible!

Having said all that, we need to be careful not to worship the music itself. God does not need entertainment; He is seeking true worshippers to worship Him in spirit and in truth. Music is a means to an end, so we must not lose sight of the 'end' because we are too focused on the 'means.' Although music inherently has a 'performance' element to it, as ministers of the Gospel of Jesus Christ, we must be sincere in the motives and intents of our heart to use the vehicle of music to draw closer to the Father and draw others to the Father. That must be our highest priority. Our focus is to seek God first as instructed in **Matthew 6:33**. Worship music ought to glorify God, edify us; the believers, and encourage non-believers to seek God. The greatest value of music used in worship should be in what it says. It should be based on scripture and knowledge of the truth, and should be accompanied by a lifestyle of obedience.

Music enhances our personal and corporate worship because it enables diverse groups of people to unite as one voice, edifies the body of Christ and strengthens our faith. However, music offered from a wrong heart is unacceptable to God as **Amos 5:23** says, *"Take away from Me the noise of your songs, For I will not hear the melody of your stringed instruments."*

Below are some scriptures which support the use of music in worship:

Ephesians 5:18-21- *"And do not be drunk with wine, in which is dissipation; but be filled with the Spirit, speaking to one another in psalms and hymns and spiritual songs, singing and making melody in your heart to the Lord, giving thanks always for all things to God the Father in the name of our Lord Jesus Christ, submitting to one another in the fear of God."*
Psalm 33:2-3- *"Praise the Lord with the harp; Make melody to Him with an instrument of ten strings. Sing to Him a new song; Play skillfully with a shout of joy.*
Psalm 150:3-4- *"Praise Him with the sound of the trumpet; Praise Him with the lute and harp! Praise Him with the timbrel and dance; Praise Him with stringed instruments and flutes!"*
Psalms 81:1-4- *"Sing for joy to God our strength; shout aloud to the God of Jacob! Begin the music, strike the tambourine, play the melodious harp and lyre. Sound the ram's horn at the New Moon, and when the moon is full, on the day of our Feast; this is a decree for Israel, an ordinance of the God of Jacob."*
1 Chronicles 16:8-11- *"Give thanks to the LORD, call*

on his name; make known among the nations what he has done. Sing to him, sing praise to him; tell of all his wonderful acts. Glory in his holy name; let the hearts of those who seek the LORD rejoice. Look to the LORD and his strength; seek his face always."

PRAYER

Almighty Father, Creator of heaven and earth, God of wonders and King of glory; I come to you now in total awe of Your presence and Your sovereignty. Father I thank You for Your grace and mercy. I am filled with gratitude for Your love which knows no end. I desire to worship You because of Who You are, not just because of what You have done. Transform my desires to match Your desires O Lord. Father, I leave behind anything that stands in my way of loving You. Words are not enough to express the love I have in my heart for You and my heart's cry is to sing new songs to You daily. Teach me how to speak in psalms and hymns and spiritual songs, teach me how to sing and make melodies in my heart to You. You are my song and my joy so I offer up my worship to You now. Like incense, let Your worship permeate the atmosphere and birth revival on the earth; let Your perfect will be done in my life as I yield to You. Let this voice of worship never be stifled or silenced by the cares of life; let Your songs of worship never depart from my heart and my lips; let Your fragrance envelop me wherever I go and let Your praise continually be in my mouth. I thank You now for answered prayers in Jesus name. Amen.

IMELA
©Isabella Ogo-Uzodike (2012)

Verse 1
You formed my inward parts
You knit my heart with love
To fit into Your plan
Your perfect plan
You called me by my name
You fashioned me to be
An instrument of praise
To worship You

Chorus(Igbo Language)
Imela, Chineke Imela
Imela, Imela
(Repeat)

Verse 2
As long as I have breath
Your praise will always be
My first priority
My highest call
I live to honour You
I long to worship You
Your name to glorify
Forevermore

Chapter Nine: The Effective Worship Leader

Zechariah 4:6- *"So he answered and said to me: "This is the word of the Lord to Zerubbabel: 'Not by might nor by power, but by My Spirit,' Says the Lord of hosts."*

I believe the starting point here must be to establish who the chief audience, judge and jury is! With us humans, the word 'effective' is relative, depending on a number of variables and circumstances; for example, culture, tradition, custom, personality, environment, level of exposure, orientation, etc. Whose opinion or judgment ultimately counts when it comes to effective worship leadership? Who is worship for; or to put it in my own language, who is the "worshippee"? As an example, in my local church, we have a number of Romanians in a congregation predominantly made up of Africans. When we worship, whilst the African worship leader is loud, animated and expressive; the Romanian is more reserved, restrained and inexpressive. Does that make one more effective than the other? Ask the congregation and you will get a mixed response, but ask the One Who is being worshipped and you just might be shocked what the answer will be. I am not at all suggesting that the opinion of others should be totally ignored; I am merely saying we need to keep things in perspective.

This is a somewhat precarious subject to touch on, so I proceed with caution because the Father's ways are so much higher than our ways. **Isaiah 55:9** reads, *"For My thoughts are not your thoughts, Nor are your ways My ways," says the Lord. For as the heavens are higher than the earth, So are My ways higher than your ways, And My thoughts than your thoughts."* Our human view and understanding of other people is very limited because we look at the outward appearance, but it is only the Lord who sees the heart **(1 Samuel 16:7)**. We can't see anyone's heart to determine the intentions or motives behind their actions; moreover, what we call ineffective may be effective in the Father's eyes, so we need to be careful not to judge too harshly or write people off so quickly.

Over the years, I have read a whole load of articles and write-ups, and I have also sat through numerous workshops and seminars where people have been taught what and how they should do, say, breathe, stand, and sing when leading worship. From each and every one of these insightful sessions, I was able to glean and learn from the knowledge and experience shared; but ultimately, the person who can give me the best tips and highest training is the Master Himself; the One who the worship is for. Not only because He is the recipient of the worship, but because He KNOWS the hearts of the worshippers, and He DESIRES their worship. Dwell on that for a moment please. Now, because He desires true worshippers, He will help the worship leader to be effective if they submit to His leading and guidance.

I read something that I found quite humorous in Craig Rigney's BlogSpot. It was an article titled: **What is a Worship Leader?** He said, *"Worship leader, if your love is music, go be a great musician in Jesus' name; but don't hide behind the image of worship leader in doing so."* I laughed about it, especially the "in Jesus Name" part, but he has a very valid point. In my few years in ministry, I have found that the mix-up between love for music and love for God is rather rampant. Love for music does not equate to love for God; as a matter of fact, love for 'God's music' does not equate to love for God! The fact that one can sing beautifully doesn't mean they can casually slot into the role of a worship leader. Worship leading is a call to ministry, not a hobby or a career. It is a call to serve, and not a call for fame and glamour as we witness today.

I sound this note of warning because I have seen extremely effective song leaders who know what to do to 'move the crowd.' They have mastered the art of performance. They know how to ride the waves of euphoria, cook up an emotional tsunami and whip up a frenzy in the audience. As a matter of fact, they could be singing or saying anything; scriptural or not, interspersed with a few 'hallelujahs' and 'praise da' Lords,' and the saints would be too sensually excited to care! Many times we get carried away by the aesthetics and lose sight of the spiritual. Some people are awesome vocalists, entertainers and performers; but are they really effective worship leaders? In fact, are they 'leading worship'? If the energetic, boisterous worship leader got people all happy, pumped up and giddy with excitement by singing some well-loved, popular choruses interpolated by craftily spoken inspirational proses, have they been more effective in worship leading than the reserved, geeky worship leader who awkwardly tottered to the pulpit, read a Bible verse and solemnly led people in worship by singing some ancient hymns interjected with scripture readings? Without the frills and thrills, have they failed in their role as a worship leader?

It is important to ask these questions because we are living in times when audience (people) centered worship is the order of the day. We judge the effectiveness of worship leaders based on how successfully they impressed the congregation, how skillfully they did the riffs and runs, how they hit the high notes, how husky or sweet their voice sounded, how well they adlibbed to the songs or how popular the songs were. Whilst these can be elements that help intensify and facilitate an enjoyable worship experience; are they really a true test of an effective worship leader? I am not proffering an answer; my hope is that these questions will stimulate some thought and be a catalyst for further reflection.

I searched the scriptures in trying to determine who an effective worship leader is, and what their job should be, but did not find any clear-cut steer. As I searched, I was reminded of a passage in the Old Testament. This scripture has always fascinated my heart, and I have prayed countless times for the Lord to allow me to experience this, in my life time, on this side of eternity. The account is from **2 Chronicles 5:11-14** (AMP):

"And when the priests had come out of the Holy Place-for all the priests present had sanctified themselves, separating themselves from everything that defiles, without regard to their divisions; And all the Levites who were singers-all of those of Asaph, Heman, and Jeduthun, with their sons and kinsmen, arrayed in fine linen, having cymbals, harps, and lyres-stood at the east end of the altar, and with them 120 priests blowing trumpets; And when the trumpeters and singers were joined in unison, making one sound to be heard in praising and thanking the Lord, and when they lifted up their voice with the trumpets and cymbals and other instruments for song and praised the Lord, saying, For He is good, for His mercy and loving-kindness endure forever, then the house of the Lord was filled with a cloud, So that the priests could not stand to minister because of the cloud, for the glory of the Lord filled the house of God."

As I chewed on this passage and pondered on lessons to be learnt from this account, some nuggets of truth hit home:

1. There wasn't any mention of a worship leader.
2. The priests sanctified and separated themselves from defilement.
3. There was unity amongst the priests.
4. The singers and musicians were in unison.

5. They were all focused on one thing: praising the Lord.
6. Their posture was that of reverence and humility.

This reminded me of the account in **Acts 2:1:** *"When the Day of Pentecost had fully come, they were all with one accord in one place."* There it was again: unity and oneness of purpose. I was further reminded of the accounts in **Revelation 4, 5, 6** and **7** about worship in the throne room. There was unanimity in focus and purpose. Despite there being thousands of thousands of angels, as well as elders and creatures: they were *"saying with a loud voice"* **(Revelation 5:12)**, *"crying out with a loud voice"* **(Revelation 7:10)**. There you have it again; unity, unison and oneness of purpose.

There definitely are lessons for us to learn from these accounts. Every single dot, comma or full stop in God's written Word is deliberate. The revelation I caught from this is that the dynamics, factors and elements at play in worship leading are much bigger, wider and deeper than an individual 'worship leader." To base the perceived success or failure of a worship service (made up of a gathering of people) on the actions (or lack of action) of one person is erroneous.

Worship is too important to God to leave in the hands of one fallible human being. I believe this with all my heart. Some of the worst places a worship leader will find themselves are places of dissension, division, conflict, disunity, backbiting, gossip, envy, jealousy, unhealthy competition or places where sexual sin is rife. Such environments are not conducive for the Holy Spirit, so a worship leader will struggle to be effective!

In my own personal experience, I have had times when I have done all I knew to do. I had done the praying, the fasting, the private devotion, and the rehearsals until every note sounded near perfect. Nevertheless, when I led worship, all I felt was dryness, emptiness, nothingness; and I've walked away embarrassed and depressed! On the other hand, I have had periods when I have felt totally unprepared, scared, nervous, unsure, and spiritually dry; and the Holy Spirit has moved powerfully in the service in such a way that I was left totally stunned beyond words. Those are the moments when I know and I know and I know that God indeed is sovereign. The Holy Spirit moves as HE wills. He cannot be manipulated to fulfil our selfish schemes.

By saying this, I am not negating the need for careful preparation. Not at all! The bottom line of what I am saying is: we can share great tips, ideas, principles; but as **Psalm 127** says, *"Unless the Lord builds the house, They labour in vain who build it; Unless the Lord guards the city, The watchman stays awake in vain."* In other words, we can read all the books and get all the knowledge available; the Lord will only move according to His will and in the 'right' atmosphere. I have said all of this because I believe it is really important to keep things in perspective; the effectiveness of a worship leader is not totally dependent on the worship leader. Whilst there are principles worship leaders can apply to improve their likelihood of being effective; ultimately, the Holy Spirit has pre-eminence.

Now that we have got that out of the way, here are the definitions of 'effective.' The Oxford Dictionary defines effective as: *"Successful in producing a desired or intended result."* The Free Dictionary adds: *"Producing a strong impression or response"* to the definition. Going by Oxford Dictionary's definition, an effective worship leader then is a worship leader who is successful in producing the desired or intended result. What is the intended result? Most people would say, "To usher the congregation into the presence of God." I would personally say the intended result is to raise people's consciousness of the presence of God, and steer their focus on to Him. God's presence was already there anyway; as the Bible says when two or three are gathered together in His name, He is in their midst (See **Matthew 8:20**). The worship leader is really just a lead worshipper who sets an example to encourage others to follow. His or her job is to help them to 'come up higher.'

I like what Ed Chinn said about worship leading. He said, *"I think leading worship is like ushering…just quietly and reverently help people to find a place in the Presence."* His presence is already there; people just need to find a spot! The other great definition I found is by Bob Kauflin in his book, **Worship Matters** He defines an effective worship leader as *"A faithful worship leader magnifies the greatness of God in Jesus Christ through the power of the Holy Spirit by skillfully combining God's Word with music; thereby motivating the gathered church to proclaim the* *gospel, to cherish God's presence, and to live for God's glory."*

You cannot lead others where you have not been yourself, and you cannot give what you don't have. The best way to be an effective worship leader is to be a worshipper yourself, in the privacy of your closet and in your daily life. Partnership and intimate relationship with the Holy Spirit are the backbones of effective worship leaders. When we commune and communicate with the Holy Spirit continually, there is an outflow and overflow of that intimacy from the secret place into the congregational gathering. Flakiness won't cut it with the Holy Spirit. He can't be fake, and He can't be faked. If we want to be effective in worship, we need to know the Father for ourselves; we need to spend time with Him in prayer, in meditation and in studying of His Word; there are no short cuts. **An effective worship leader is one who is Spirit-filled and Spirit led.** It really is that simple.

In my few years in ministry, I have come across some 'worship leaders' who make statements like: "They always love my worship; whenever I lead worship, people come up to me and tell me how much I blessed them; they prefer my worship to sister so and so... blah blah blah..." By their words, they immediately show you their heart! They're in a singing competition, and it has become a popularity contest for the spiritually immature. This is a very dangerous place for any worshipper to be. When it becomes more about us than about Him, we know we're headed for trouble! This is where spiritual maturity matters in worship leading. Every one of us has an inbuilt antenna which loves and responds to affirmation; we like to be appreciated; we like to be accepted and celebrated. That's absolutely understandable, but when the praises and flattering tongues of men become our motivators, it becomes a stronghold like a drug to an addict, and it needs to be broken immediately!

As I shared at the beginning of this book, I began to lead worship 'by default.' I didn't have an inkling of what leading worship was about. Yes, I knew I loved the Lord with all my heart, and I loved to be in His presence, but that was it. I loved to worship, but I was a spiritual babe. I have to confess, I was excited about the word 'leader' because the leader is the boss; I can tell people what to do and how to do it! But you and I know it is not so in the Kingdom of God. In the Kingdom, we are servant leaders; we serve those we lead. This is one of the greatest issues plaguing the church today – titles without training; positions without preparation! I am talking about spiritual training and preparation here. Jesus Christ is our prime example. Inspiring, eloquent, charismatic have now been misinterpreted to mean anointed and appointed. Think about the stuttering Moses and the articulate Aaron; who do you imagine would have been the people's choice to go speak to Pharaoh on their behalf? But God chose the least qualified in the eyes of men.

I have extensively shared my thoughts on the lifestyle of a worshipper, so there is no need to repeat everything here. The worship leader is first and foremost a worshipper, so their lifestyle should line up their title; their walk should line up with their talk. And yes, it is possible to be effective in worship leading without being a great singer. This point is pertinent because I have come across churches where the worship leader has been chosen based on their vocal prowess. There is no doubt that being able to hold a note is definitely a strength and advantage which adds to the versatility of a worship leader, but being a good singer is not tantamount to being a good worship leader. In the reality of our culture and orientation, it would be near impossible to be an effective worship leader in this time and age without any musical ability; however we must recognize that good singing does not equal effective worship leading.

It is important and indeed needful to ensure we prepare properly for worship leading; we need to choose the appropriate songs for the service, rehearse the songs, pray, ensure the sounds, lighting, atmosphere, and temperatures are right. You'd be shocked at how much a room that is too hot or too cold can take away from the worship experience. By setting the right atmosphere, we eliminate, or at least reduce the potentials for distractions during the service.

In doing all of this, we must keep sight of the truth that the worship is to the Father and for His enjoyment. The worship leader prepares the people's heart for worship and steers their attention away from their cares, worries, distractions and concerns to the awesomeness and worthiness of the Father. The congregation are not the recipients of worship; they are the givers of worship, so we cannot base the effectiveness on how much they 'enjoyed' the experience.

As mentioned earlier, human beings are creatures of habit; we have our personal styles and preferences; your perception is different from mine, and who you consider to be an effective worship leader may be far from my reality. The focus of worship is the Father; not our tastes, style, opinions, and so on. If we want to be effective, we have to prioritize spending quality time in God's presence.

In closing, let us heed Apostle Paul's counsel in **Romans 8:3-8:**
"*For I say, through the grace given to me, to everyone who is among you, not to think of himself more highly than he ought to think, but to think soberly, as God has dealt to each one a measure of faith. For as we have many members in one body, but all the members do not have the same function, so we, being many, are one body in Christ, and individually members of one another. Having then gifts differing according to the grace that is given to us, let us use them: if prophecy, let us prophesy in proportion to our faith; or ministry, let us use it in our ministering; he who teaches, in teaching; he who exhorts, in exhortation; he who gives, with liberality; he who leads, with diligence; he who shows mercy, with cheerfulness.*"

PRAYER

Father, I thank You for everything You have taught me through this section on worship leading, I now ask for Your help to be a more effective worshipper for I know that I cannot give what I do not have. Dear Lord, help me to love Your glory more than the fleeting praise of men.Keep my heart fixed on You, keep my eyes focussed on You and keep me from falling into the trap of pride or self-exaltation. Holy Spirit, You are the best Teacher and Helper; please help me to love You and Your people more than the songs I sing; keep me genuine in my walk with You; mold me into a lead worshipper so that my passion for You will stir up the spirit of worship and attract others to seek You more and worship You more everyday. Father, help me to value Your Word above the opinions of man and to seek You earnestly with my whole heart. Destroy every iota of carnal-mindedness and self-seeking motives, and keep my intentions pure at all times. Lord, help me to walk in character and to lay down every selfish desire in serving You. Thank You for Your love and grace. I thank You because Your grace is sufficient for me and Your joy is my strength. May Your name be forever praised in Jesus name. Amen.

FOR YOUR LOVE
©Isabella Ogo-Uzodike (2012)

Verse 1
For Your love, I'm willing to pay the price
For Your love, I'm willing to sacrifice
For Your love, I'm willing to lose my pride
For Your love, for Your love

Verse 2
For Your love, I'm willing to take the test
For Your love, I'm willing to do my best
For Your love, I'm willing to change my ways
For Your love, for Your love

Chorus
I pledge my love to You
I give my heart to You
Lay down my will for You
For You my Love

Bridge
I'll stay faithful and true
Devoted to You
Never give up on You

Chapter Ten: Conclusion...Now What?

James 1:22–25 *"But be doers of the word, and not hearers only, deceiving yourselves. For if anyone is a hearer of the word and not a doer, he is like a man observing his natural face in a mirror; for he observes himself, goes away, and immediately forgets what kind of man he was. But he who looks into the perfect law of liberty and continues in it, and is not a forgetful hearer but a doer of the work, this one will be blessed in what he does."*

I suppose the question at this time is, "NOW WHAT?" We have defined worship, or rather attempted to define worship; looked at the relationship between praise and worship, talked about the Holy Spirit, identified the qualities that make the lifestyle of a worshipper, learnt about David, and considered the whats, whys, wheres, whens and hows of worship and worship leading; so what's next?

It is time to stand on the Word and put everything learnt into practice. When it comes to spiritual matters, head knowledge without heart knowledge can be likened to having an expensive exquisite automobile without a key. You can admire it, describe it, boast about it; but you can't access it, drive it or enjoy it! It would be great to know that you enjoyed reading this book, but if all you got from it was enjoyment, this would all have been in vain. It would be great to hear that some of the personal stories I shared in this book entertained you, but if all you got from this book was entertainment, the book is better not written at all.

The sole purpose and overriding objective for writing this book is to equip you; the reader, with the knowledge to stir up the worshipper in you, to rouse your heart of worship, to ignite your passion for the Father so that you become a worshipper after the Father's heart. The Father's desire is that we single-mindedly worship Him in spirit and in truth. And that is the starting point: DESIRE. I believe you picked up this book because there is a DESIRE in your heart to be a worshipper after the Father's heart. Desire; some say, is the starting point of all accomplishment. **Psalm 37:4** says, *"Delight yourself also in the Lord, and He shall give you the desires of your heart."*

I would love to be prescriptive and say to you, "There you have it! Now you are fully equipped to worship the Father in spirit and in truth." But the truth is that NO MAN can really teach you how to worship God and how to be a worshipper after the Father's heart. Only the Father; through the Son, with the help of the Holy Spirit can truly teach you and reveal His heart to you. Only the Father who created you knows what He put inside of You; He knows what makes you tick; He knows how to get your attention; He knows how to draw you close, and He knows how to correct and counsel you in a way no man can. He knows just the right amount of pressure to exert that will be effective, and yet not drive you round the bend; He knows how to bring you to your knees; He knows how to touch your heart so that you can touch His. So ask the Father to teach you. Cry out as David did in **Psalm 25:4-5:** *"Show me Your ways, O Lord; Teach me Your paths. Lead me in Your truth and teach me, For You are the God of my salvation; On You I wait all the day."* And true to His Word, I earnestly believe that you will find Him when you seek Him with all your heart in line with His Word in **Jeremiah 29:13:** *"And you will seek Me and find Me, when you search for Me with all your heart."*

My children all have my DNA and my husband's DNA. They have all grown up in the same household, ate the same food, were taught the same principles, and yet; they're all so different. As a mother, I KNOW each of my children, and I know what approach to take when I need to get their attention. To one, I offer food and that gets his attention straight away. If I did the same with the other three, I'd be wasting my time. To another, I offer money as a reward. In discipline, to one I take away her telephone, and that gets her attention; to another, her telephone makes no difference whatsoever. Taking away her phone is no deterrent because she does not need her telephone. That is how the Father is with us; He KNOWS us more than anyone else will ever know us, even more than we know ourselves.

In the same vein, my children KNOW me. They know what to do to make me happy, and they know what NOT to do. When they want to please me, they deliberately do certain things like tidy my bedroom or wash dishes without being asked. They telephone me from wherever they are and just say they called to check up on me. They work hard at school and come home with good grades. They know me, so they know what pleases me and what displeases me. The same applies even in a marriage; the spouses learn each other's ways in order to have a successful marriage. We learn about our likes and dislikes, our preferences and our 'pet peeves,' our strengths and weaknesses so that we can work together to make the best of our relationship.

This is the same with the Father. The more we spend time with Him, the more we will know Him; and the more we know Him, the more we will know the things which please and displease Him. We will move on from knowing about Him to knowing Him. As stated earlier in the book, knowing about someone is NOT the same as knowing someone. **John 17:3** says, *"And this is eternal life, that they may __know You__, the only true God, and Jesus Christ whom You have sent."* Knowing Him is more than memorising and quoting scriptures. Those with really good memories can cram and regurgitate scriptures without revelation. That is purely head knowledge; intellectual, at its best with little or no life-transforming potential. **John 8:32** says, *"And you will know the truth, and the truth will set you FREE!"* It is not enough to just know the truth; we need to DO the truth we know. It is the truth we know and do that will set us free. I liken it to *Logos;* the "written Word" of God, and *Rhema;* the "spoken Word" of God. God's Word is potent and stands true in all circumstances and for all situations, as **Hebrews 4:12** says, *"For the word of God is living and powerful, and sharper than any two-edged sword, piercing even to the division of soul and spirit, and of joints and marrow, and is a discerner of the thoughts and intents of the heart."* Nevertheless, unless you get a revelation from the Holy Spirit on how to correctly apply the Word to and in your specific situation, it sits pretty and remains just what it is: a written Word!

Why should I worship God? We looked at all the Biblical reasons in a previous chapter, but how about moving past man's religion, and all the associated rituals, to say I worship Him simply **BECAUSE I LOVE HIM** more than I love anything or anyone else, and I want to please Him. In loving Him, all law is fulfilled! I worship Him because we are in a deep, intimate loving relationship which compares to no other! The sole purpose of worship must always be to please God; the essence of worship is to pleasure God! Man's chief end is to glorify God forever. Let's worship God because He is God. Period. End of story.

Where should I worship God? The Father really doesn't mind where we worship Him; He just loves our worship. He doesn't need a precise building, a specific location, a particular spot, or an exact room. We have the liberty to worship the Father **EVERYWHERE** and **ANYWHERE.** Whether in church, at home, at work, in school, in the gym, driving, cooking, walking, running, in a restaurant, in the privacy of our bedroom, even in the rest room;

worship offered from a pure and humble heart based on His Word and precepts is acceptable to the Father.

When should I worship God? The Father desires for us to worship Him **AT ALL TIMES AND IN ALL SEASONS.** It doesn't have to be during a certain hour, only on specific days, during a worship service, or in congregational gatherings; but worship is an unrestricted flow of adoration, which permeates every aspect of our life and exudes from the very core of our being. Our worship is not dependent on our feelings, conditions or circumstances. Our life should flow in ceaseless worship through all the seasons of life. We all have our summers, springs, winters and autumns of life; and each season brings with it challenges, tests and trials. There is a lot to learn from David, who despite the countless obstacles and devastation he faced, consistently worshipped God.

How should I worship God? Jesus Christ simply says in **John 4:24**, "They that worship Him must worship Him **IN SPIRIT AND IN TRUTH.**" It's more than the great worship music; it's more than the lifting of holy hands; it's more than the tears rolling down our faces; it's more than the clapping of hands, or the shouting of "Hallelujah!" It is more than lying on the floor; it's bigger than the big choir and huge church orchestras; it's higher than the shrill voice of the wonderful sopranos and deeper than the smooth crooning of the *basso profundo*. These are all expressions, and indeed integral aspects of our worship experience, but they are not worship. True worship is that of the spirit man. In worship, the condition of the heart is everything.

In the section, '*Worship that Pleases God*' in the book, **The Purpose Driven Life**, Rick Warren suggests: *"The best style of worship is the one that most authentically represents your love for God, based on the background and personality God gave you."* Rick Warren observes, *"There is no 'one-size-fits-all' approach to worship and friendship with God. One thing is certain. You don't bring glory to God by trying to be someone God never intended you to be. God wants you to be yourself. It's who you are and the way you live that counts before God. That's the kind of people the Father is out looking for: those who are simply and honestly themselves before him in their worship."*

In closing, remember what I said in the first chapter about the four key aspects of successful Christian living, which will always keep us focused on the Father and His Kingdom. We all need to commit these four principles to memory and evaluate our daily actions based on them. I encourage us to always remember these points and use the questions below as a litmus test for everything we think, do and say on a daily basis. We ought to ask ourselves these four questions:

1. **Worship:** Does it enhance my worship of the Father?
2. **Discipline:** Does it demonstrate a disciplined life?
3. **Ministry:** Does it minister life to others?
4. **Evangelism:** Does it help spread the Good News of Jesus Christ?

Each and every one of us must be resolute in our decision to make any lifestyle changes. There will be trials; there will be temptations; there will be tests and tribulations, but we must single-mindedly decide to STAND on God's Word and to STAND with God. The Holy Spirit is our ever-present Help, so we can always rely on His help in every situation.

As I conclude this book, I pray for you today as Paul prayed in **Colossians 1:9-10:** *"...that you may be filled with the knowledge of His will in all wisdom and spiritual understanding; that you may walk worthy of the Lord, fully pleasing Him, being fruitful in every good work and increasing in the knowledge of God."*

PRAYER

Gracious Father, I thank You for everything You have taught me through this book, and I thank You for Your grace to implement the changes needed in my life. I know I cannot make the changes by my own strength, but I fully rely on the help and counsel of Your Holy Spirit, being confident of this very thing: that You Who began this good work in me will complete it until the day of Jesus Christ. Amen.

I WAIT FOR YOU
©Isabella Ogo-Uzodike (2009)

Verse 1
As the deer pants for the water brooks
I long for You
As the bride yearns for her bridegroom
I long for You

Chorus
I wait for You
I wait for You
In eager anticipation
In hopeful expectation
In humble adoration
I wait for You my Love
I wait for You
I wait for You
In humble adoration
I wait for You my Love

Verse 2
More than signs, more than the wonders
I long for You
More than fame, more than the glamour
I long for You

Bridge
Even so, come Lord Jesus come
Even so, let Your Kingdom come
Even so, come Lord Jesus come
Even so, let Your will be done

Other resources from the Author:

Lost Without You (Audio CD)

A collection of 12 original contemporary worship songs

Heaven's Anthem (Audio CD)

A collection of 12 original contemporary worship songs

My Tori Don Change (Audio CD)

A collection of ten original Afro-Gospel songs

These songs can be downloaded from iTunes, Amazon, CD Baby and other online music outlets

For more information, please visit www.isabellamelodies.com

www.ingramcontent.com/pod-product-compliance
Lightning Source LLC
Chambersburg PA
CBHW071529040426
42452CB00008B/943